D1198751

Copyright © 2018 Compilation and arrangement by Brian Coleman

Book and cover design by James Blackwell, www.BlackwellSpace.com

Published in the United States by Wax Facts Press, Everett, MA.

Coleman, Brian
Buy Me, Boston. Local Ads and Flyers, 1960s – 1980s. Volume 1.

ISBN 978-0-9903076-6-2

Library of Congress Control Number: 2018906415

Printed and bound in the United States of America

Book cover photo © 1986 by Larry Bouchie, www.TurboPR.com.
Modified with permission.

This book, and its author and publisher, are not affiliated with, endorsed by, or sponsored by the artists or publishers of the materials collected herein.

www.BuyMeBoston.com
www.BrianColemanBooks.com
www.Instagram.com/DignifiedAndOld

IMPORTANT NOTE: Many of the objects featured in this book were found in defunct publications or handbills without attribution, so many of the creators behind them could not be identified. We believe that this publication constitutes fair use of all materials featured, and is not an infringement of copyright under the Copyright Act, 17 U.S.C. § 107. However, if you have any rights to any of these visuals and do not wish to be included, you have our sincere apologies and we will remove your work from all future printings.

Let us know at Hello@GoodRoadGoods.com.

Never-ending THANKS for friendship, inspiration, assistance ... and for letting me rifle through your stuff:

David Bieber

Chuck White

Kay Bourne

Wayne Valdez

Reebee Garofalo

Peter Prescott

Duane Lucia

Russ Gershon

Tristram Lozaw

To James Blackwell, my steady collaborator, on yet another wacky book. Thanks for the hard work and killer visuals.

To Pacey Foster of the Massachusetts Hip-Hop Archive at UMass Boston; and Jim Botticelli of Dirty Old Boston – two friends who have inspired me with their own archival zeal and accomplishments.

To Dan Booth and Adam DeFalco, for lending ears and legal expertise, and for friendship and encouragement.

To Chuck, Lance and the crew at the David Bieber Archives, for never locking the door and turning off the lights when you saw me coming...

And, as always, to my amazing wife Margot. Sorry about the piles of newspapers and magazines ... I'll clean them up soon, I promise.

A NOTE FROM THE CURATOR

I will start with a not-so-scandalous admission: I am *not* a born-and-bred Bostonian. But I have lived here for more years of my life than any other place, so at the very least I consider myself a stepson of this wacky and beautiful town.

This book is the result of dozens, maybe hundreds, of hours of research; scanning; visiting the homes and storage space stashes of important Boston archivists; more scanning; and leafing through my own piles of media gathered over the past 30 years. And, of course, more scanning after that.

All images in this tome are scanned from original sources, not from Google Images or any other online shortcut. Some pages jump out in crisp, brilliant color; others are tattered and yellowed with age. But it's all *real*.

The thing I have always loved about advertisements (including event flyers and posters) is that they are the most direct and honest way that any undertaking – whether it's a theater troupe, a band, a restaurant or a hair salon – has to communicate with the public. Advertisements are not mediated by journalists or editors. They contain exactly what the owner wants to say. Sometimes ads are a mess; sometimes they are beautiful and/or clever. There is no right way to place an ad, but I have always respected anyone who tries.

Importantly (to me, at least), almost every ad in this book was placed in an independent media outlet. I have generally tried to steer clear of our town's bigger, more corporate

ATTENTION AUTHORS!

Now it is possible to produce your own book — complete from typesetting to printing — at a competitive price. Authors Services, a division of Educational Publishers, can provide the necessary talent to put your poetry, music, novels, or technical material in a complete book. Write **Mr. John Yirrell** today at Educational Publishers. Box 117, Reading, MA 01867.

publications in these pages, because there is a much higher barrier of entry. The easier it is to afford (relatively speaking, of course), the more chance there is that smaller, mom-and-pop businesses can scrape together nickels and dimes to place an ad.

Some readers may lament the lack of information given on each page, aside from the image source and year. To be clear: *Buy Me, Boston* is not meant as an academic treatise, or an exhaustive, comprehensive survey of our local and regional media over the past half century. It is simply a stroll through Boston – and, occasionally, its surrounding areas – from one person's vantagepoint. I want people to summon their own memories, and maybe even dig into some of this history for themselves.

As I perused any given media source, my gaze would wander in quite unpredictable ways. Sometimes I was drawn in by an image, or a font used. Sometimes a clear memory slapped me in the face as I gazed upon a logo or date, bringing me back to a club or bar that I frequented when I myself arrived here three decades ago.

All in all, I have tried to show an honest and inclusive overview of our city. I have made a conscious effort to include businesses, people and events that haven't gotten a lot of exposure in other local archival endeavors I have seen. Clubs like the Western Front, Roscoe's, The Middle East, Lane's of Mattapan and Jack's; legendary neighborhood anchors like A Nubian Notion and Skippy White's Records; events sponsored by the Boston Negro Artists' Association, the Elma Lewis School of Fine Arts, and Northeastern University's AAMARP; and Jack's Autobody & Paint in Hyde Park ("Boston's first gay owned, staffed and operated body shop.")

I am a lifelong music fanatic, so the book is unavoidably skewed towards that side of Boston's history. But I have also tried to expand into many other areas. That being said, music always draws me in, and I make no excuses.

Finally, as you can see in the title of the book, this is Volume 1. That means there is plenty more to share from my stockpile of physical and scanned items, if people are supportive of these efforts. If you like what you see, please let me know, and tell a friend, too. Better yet, if you have some goods to share for Volume 2, I have a scanner and will travel.

Thanks for hearing me out, and now… ENJOY!

Brian Coleman
Revere, MA
www.BrianColemanBooks.com

PLEASE CHECK OUT MY FRIENDS AND ARCHIVAL INSPIRATIONS AT THESE URLS:

David Bieber Archives
www.DavidBieberArchives.com

Kay Bourne Archives
www.Emerson.edu/library/archives/special-collections

Wayne Valdez
www.instagram.com/WayneValdez

Reebee Garofalo
www.Reebee.net

Duane Lucia and Gallery East
www.GalleryEastNetwork.com

Dirty Old Boston
www.Facebook.com/DirtyOldBoston

Massachusetts Hip-Hop Archive at UMass Boston
http://openarchives.umb.edu/cdm/landingpage/collection/p15774coll30

Cornell Hip Hop Collection
http://rmc.library.cornell.edu/hiphop/index.html

Rushtown 298 [Prime Minister Pete Nice]
www.instagram.com/Rushtown298

Chris Veltri / Groove Merchant Records
www.instagram.com/CollageDropoutSF

Boston University News
October 21, 1971
[David Bieber Archives]

Boston Advertiser
Nov 24, 1963
[Author's collection]

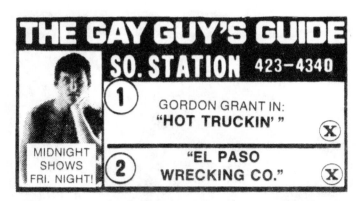

THE GAY GUY'S GUIDE

SO. STATION 423-4340

1 GORDON GRANT IN:
"HOT TRUCKIN' " **X**

MIDNIGHT SHOWS FRI. NIGHT!

2 "EL PASO WRECKING CO." **X**

Boston's Best All Male Show!

art 1
204 TREMONT ST. BOSTON 482-4661

X-RATED ALL MALE CAST

5 HOUR MARATHON!

LEVIS & LEATHER
INITIATION RIGHTS
BUSY BOYS
LEATHER NARCISSUS
BITTERSWEET

Boston
Phoenix
July 4, 1978
[David Bieber Archives]

art 2
204 TREMONT ST. BOSTON
482-4661

TWO ADULT HITS

X

Continuous from 10AM

*I got those
Iced Denim blues . . .
and why not?*

the feelin's appealin'

It was born to be worn.
Dyed and tried.
Ready to let loose
this fall
in jeans and jackets
and yes, a dress (or two).
It's faded
but fast and furious.
Go on, get it . . .
get the feeling.

Iced Denim. Specially treated for a wild, worn, and wonderful look. This fall, it's everywhere. Here, from the collection: Area Code Iced Denim fitted dress for Juniors. With zip front, double stitch detailing and cinched bodice. Sizes 3–13. $112.
Juniors — all Filene's stores.

feeling
FILENE'S

Boston Magazine
August 1987
[David Bieber Archives]

Boston Tea Party flyer
March 1967
[David Bieber Archives]

ROUTE ONE, SAUGUS

Red Sox program
1987
[Author's collection]

Sugar Shack

110 Boylston Street
426-0086
Presents

SHOWTIMES
10 pm & 1 am

Sept. 23
TAVARES

Sept. 30 - Oct. 6
JOHNNY TAYLOR

Oct. 7 - Oct. 13
SOUL CHILDREN

Sept. 16 - 22
FUNKADELIC PARLIAMENT

for further
information call:
426-1289

Real Paper
September 18, 1974
[Author's Collection]

Boston Rock magazine
February 1982
[Author's collection]

THIS IS BOSTON *NOT L.A.!*

DECADENCE
THE FREEZE
THE F.U.'s
GANG GREEN
THE GROINOIDS
JERRY'S KIDS
THE PROLETARIAT
An LP Coming Soon!

photo: Phil In Phlash

Modern Method 012

Boston Magazine
July 1979
[David Bieber Archives]

Too close for comfort?

If you try to hide your face because of unwanted hairs, then you haven't tried Depilatron in Brookline.

Depilatron's method is painless, and can be used to remove unwanted hair from all parts of the body. There's no fear of irritation and you can put on make-up immediately after treatment.

Instead of trying to hide your face because of unwanted hairs, come to one of our licensed technicians for **a free consultation and a free ten-minute introductory treatment.**

So if your unwanted hair makes you uncomfortable, think about Depilatron...before you get too close.

Depilatron
of New England, Inc.

1290 Beacon St. (at Coolidge Corner), Brookline, MA
Office Hours — Monday-Saturday, 8:30 am-9 pm.
734-1874 or 734-1814   Physician Supervised

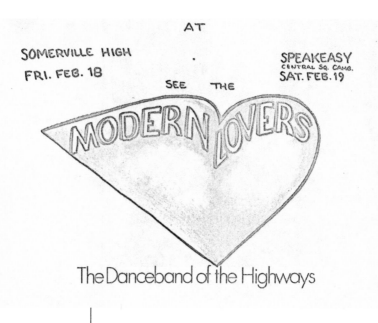

Concert flyer (photocopied)
February 1972
[David Bieber Archives]

Concert flyer

May 1982

[Courtesy of Gallery East Productions]

ELLA

ONLY BOSTON CONCERT

symphony hall sunday may 14
8:30

$5 $7.50 $10 $15
1/2 tax deductible
phone: **742-7466**
266-1492

**ALL PROCEEDS BENEFIT
EYE RESEARCH**

ELLA FITZGERALD is donating
her time and her talent for this
RETINA FOUNDATION benefit
in the battle against blindness.

Boston After Dark

May 2, 1972

[David Bieber Archives]

Concert flyer

July 1979

[Kay Bourne Archives at Emerson College:
Iwasaki Library, Special Collections.]

COCA COLA, CALLENDER FUEL, INC. and MAURICE STARR PRODUCTIONS

presents the

FIRST ANNUAL
BOSTON BLACK MUSIC AWARDS
and BLACK ACHIEVERS PRESENTATION

FRIDAY, JULY 10, 1987
STRAND THEATRE
DORCHESTER, MASS.

INSIDE PHOTOS INCLUDE:
NEW EDITIONS
SUPERIORS
MAURICE STARR
NEW KIDS
ON THE BLOCK

Program front cover

July 10, 1987

[Kay Bourne Archives at Emerson College:
Iwasaki Library, Special Collections.]

BEAUTIFUL YOUNG LADIES WILL PAMPER YOU BREATHLESS AT
SWEDISH SAUNA

Enjoy the pleasures of an imperial body massage. Large authentic rock sauna room, Eucalyptus decongestant chamber, infrared lamps to soothe nerves, Miami sun rooms, whirlpool featuring therapeutic massage, imperial bubble bath (excluding Reading) and free refreshments in our Bachelor Lounge

Location	Address	Information	Appointment
READING, MA.	125 Main Street	(617) 944-7395	(617) 944-7469
PEABODY, MA.	Rear of Newbury Plaza	(617) 535-4804	(617) 535-4999
WARWICK, R.I.	8 Airport Plaza	(401) 738-4950	(401) 738-4650
MANCHESTER, N.H.	73 Lowell Street	(603) 669-9010	(603) 669-0183
HARTFORD, CT	80 Pratt Street	(203) 247-0065	(203) 247-9580

ANNOUNCES OUR NEW LOCATION

PROVIDENCE, R.I.	101 Dyer Street	(401) 831-7849	(401) 831-1848

TRY THE ULTIMATE EXPERIENCE
Open 11 A.M. - 12 Mid. 7 Days a Week Appointments preferred, but not necessary

Night Time magazine

January 1975

[David Bieber Archives]

Hospital Clogs

Danish Clogs w/backs

ESKiL'S Clog Shop

Boston's Largest Selection of Clogs

For Men, Women & Children

Made In Sweden

353-0685

50 Styles & colors to choose from. Sizes to fit the entire family

475 Comm. Ave., Boston (Between Mass. Ave. and Kenmore Sq.)
HYANNIS - PROVINCETOWN - NORTH CONWAY, NH

CARMEN'S PLACE

Fresh-Squeezed Juice
Sandwiches ● Salads
Fresh Fruit Frozen Yogurts
Haagen-Dasz Ice Cream
Tropical Fruit Smoothies

52 Boylston St.
(Harvard Sq.)   OPEN 7 DAYS A WEEK

160 Prospect St.
(betw. Central & Inman Sq.)

**Shelly's Dance School
Now in Kenmore Sq.**

How many times have you said —
"I wish I could dance like that"?
Now you can. Disco classes starting throughout July.
Learn the latest in partner dancing with many turns
and the freak. 6 wks. $35.00 Call now 236-1868

Private instruction available.

720 Beacon St., Boston — **236-1868**

July 3
Richie Havens

IN CONCERT Monday, July 3
2 Shows: 9 & 11 P.M.
Special Guests: JEANIE STAHL & MASON DARING

July 6, 7 & 8 - ESTES BOYS
July 12, 13, 14 & 15 - BRANCH BROTHERS

Headliners North.

Tickets at Boxoffice & Ticketron
Advanced Tickets $5.50
at Ticketron & Swifts
Take Exit 7E off Rt.3
ONLY 40 Minutes from Boston

In Railroad Square,
Nashua, N.H.
(603)889-8844

In the heart of Downtown Nashua in Railroad Square
NEXT to the Chart House

We will buy your records!

ZOUNDZ!

New, used and rare LPs at the lowest prices, the highest cash paid and the fairest trade-in allowances for your unwanted long playing records.

ZOUNDZ! Everything you need in a record store is at 845 Boylston St., Boston (across from Pru) 267-2555

Open Every Day
All Records Guaranteed

Beggars Banquet Records **661-7731**

**65 MT. AUBURN
HARVARD SQ.
CAMBRIDGE**

Records Bought & Sold

- **Much more cash trade-in for your records**
- **Friendly Service**
- **Best in used "like new" records**
- **Double, triple your music dollar**
- **Collectors items**

**HOURS
MON-WED 10-9
THURS-FRI 10-10
SAT 9-6 SUN 12-6**

[David Bieber Archives] | July 4, 1978 | *Boston Phoenix*

Concert poster
June 1980
[Courtesy of Russ Gershon]

Kenmore Comet newspaper
October 18, 1984
[Wayne Valdez Archives]

Boston Phoenix
December 1, 1981
[David Bieber Archives]

The best walking tour of Boston is 740 feet above the ground.

That's because our whole tour of Boston begins and ends in the Hancock Tower Observatory on the 60th floor, atop the tallest building in New England.

See the most spectacular view of Boston there is, with 60 miles of breathtaking scenery. Then experience the Boston of 200 years ago through our unique multi-media exhibits. Like a photorama of Massachusetts' rich historical heritage. A show about Boston in 1775, featuring a 20-foot scale model. And a lot more.

The Observatory is open Monday through Saturday from 9am to 11pm, and Sundays from noon till 11pm, every day except Thanksgiving and Christmas. Admission is $1.50 for adults, 75¢ for children 5 through 15. Group and Convention rates are available: call 247-1976. Our ticket office is located on St. James Avenue opposite Copley Square.

Visit the Hancock Tower Observatory. It's a walking tour of Boston that's pleasing to the eye—and easy on the feet. **John Hancock Observatory**
The Best Place to See Boston.

View July 4th holiday festivities from our Observatory. Open 9am, Sun. 7/2.

Boston Phoenix
July 4, 1978
[David Bieber Archives]

AAMARP
VISUAL & PERFORMING ARTS COMPLEX AT NORTHEASTERN UNIVERSITY
11 LEON STREET
BOSTON, MASSACHUSETTS
APRIL 1-30, 1981
PAINTINGS, DRAWINGS, SCULPTURE
•1981•
CATALOG PRINTED COURTESY OF SIMMONS COLLEGE

Front cover of catalog

April 1981

[Kay Bourne Archives at Emerson College: Iwasaki Library, Special Collections.]

16 April 1970

IN PERSON
MELVIN
VAN PEEBLES

Friday, April 17
8:00 p.m.

ROXBURY CINEMA
Cor. Waverly & Warren Sts.

NOW PLAYING
VAN PEEBLES'
"THREE DAY PASS"
LEROI JONES'
"DUTCHMAN"

Bay State Banner

April 1970

[Kay Bourne Archives at Emerson College: Iwasaki Library, Special Collections.]

 **BOB MARLEY
and the
WAILERS**

**PATTI
LABELLE**   **EDDIE
PALMIERI**

OLATUNJI   JABULA

with special guest

DICK GREGORY

Harvard Stadium Saturday, July 21, 1979
12:00 NOON–6:00 P.M.
Raindate, July 22

Advance Ticket Sales: $10.00 in the stands
$12.00 on the lawn
Day of the Concert: $12.00 in the stands
$14.00 on the lawn

Advance Tickets available at: all Ticketron Outlets, Nubian Notion, and
Strawberries.
Tickets on day of the concert available at Harvard Stadium Box Office only.

AMANdla is presented by HAYMARKET CONCERTS in
cooperation with ENGLISH PRODUCTIONS, INC.

Concert poster

July 1979

[Courtesy of Reebee Garofalo]

Boston After Dark
October 1, 1969
[David Bieber Archives]

RATHSKELLAR

528 Commonwealth Ave., Kenmore Sq., Boston

Grand Opening

Wednesday, Sept. 25

featuring

"Phluph"

COMING SUNDAY, SEPTEMBER 29 2 P.M.-ON

New England Talent Showcase

HEARTS	LIVE LOBSTER
QUICK	DEAD END KIDS
RUN DRY	PHLUPH
CHRIS MARTIN GROUP	HOBO TOAD
FOX FIRE	WILEY CRAWFORD GROUP

Owned & Operated by Jim Harold & Fred Loder

Night Time magazine
September 1974
[David Bieber Archives]

THE RAT

BOSTON ROCK & ROLL
528 COMM. AVE.
BOSTON, MASS. 02215
617-247-7713

Mon.-Tues.
Mar. 7th-8th
Orchestra Luna

Wed., March 9th
Max Ferguson Band

Thurs.-Fri.
March 10th-11th
Willie Loco Alexander and His Boom Boom Band
and
Infliktors

Sat.-Sun.
March 12th-13th
Real Kids
and
Nervous Eaters

Mon.-Wed.
March 14th-16th
Mercury Recording Artists
The
RUNA-WAYS
w/Mon. **Real Kids**
Tues. **Reddy Teddy**
Wed. **Thundertrain**
Runaway reservations held until 8:30 P.M.

Live Rat LP • Double Rock — $8.95 &
.75 handling • **$9.74**
Rat Records "A" • 528 Comm. Ave.,
Boston, MA

[March 1977]

THE RAT

BOSTON ROCK & ROLL
528 COMM. AVE.
BOSTON, MASS. 02215
(617) 247-7713

MON.
STOMPERS
&
BUSTERS

TUES.
INFLIKTORS
&
SPECIAL GUEST

WED.
EASTWOOD PIKE
&
PHANTOMS

THURS.-
SUN.

THEY'RE
BACK!

THUNDERTRAIN   THUNDERTRAIN

&
ROMANTICS

[July 1978]

THE CHANNEL

Boston's Largest Concert
& Dance Club
Located directly on the Waterfront!

Fri. Sept. 5
**THE ATLANTICS
LA PESTE
2X4's**

Thurs. Sept. 11
**MIDNIGHT TRAVELLER
STOLEN KISSES**

Fr. Sept. 12
**BALLOON • THE EGGS
THE MODES
THE MAKE**

Thurs. Sept. 18
**THE MUNDANES
THE TWEEDS**

Fri. Sept. 19
**PASTICHE
ARTHUR SLICK
& THE NICE GIRLS**

Sat. Sept. 20
PUNK JAZZ...
JAMES BLOOD ULMER

Thurs. Sept. 25
**LOU MIAMI &
THE KOZMETIX**
WITH BIG WORLD

Fri. Sept. 26
**THE STOMPERS
THE GAMES**

Advance Ticket Sales! All Strawberries • Out of Town. Harvard Sq. • Open Door in Brockton • Concert Charge • 426-8181 • Elsie's

LARGE GAME ROOM
LOW DRINK PRICES
New concert line: 451-1905 ID's required
Across the bridge from South Station.
Turn right at first light.

25 Necco Street, 451-1050.

[September 1980]

THE CHANNEL

THE ONLY
PLACE TO ROCK!

BOSTON'S BEST LIVE ROCK

Wed July 6 WBOS	Arista Recording Artists # Ministry Blackouts
Fri 8	**Neighborhoods** Peter Dayton • Prime Movers
Sun 10 **All Ages!** **3 p.m.**	# Bad Brains 007 • Psycho
Wed 13	Viper • The Steps • Exports • Dorian Grey
Sat 16	**Waitresses** Our Daughters Wedding Til Tuesday
Sat 23	**Enemy • Reflectors**
Sun 24 **All Ages!** **3 p.m.**	# Angry Samoans Moving Targets

25 Necco St. Boston 451-1905
ID'S REQUIRED

ADVANCE TICKETS • ALL STRAWBERRIES • OUT OF TOWN
HARVARD SQUARE • OPEN DOOR BROCKTON • NEWBURY COMICS • TICKETRON

[July 1983]

Concert poster

September 1970

[Kay Bourne Archives at Emerson College:
Iwasaki Library, Special Collections.]

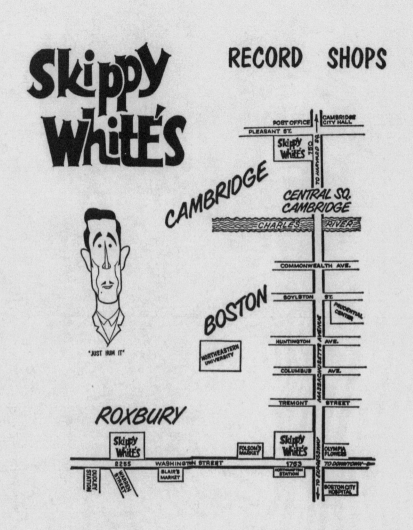

Miss Black Fox program ad

June 1975

[Kay Bourne Archives at Emerson College:
Iwasaki Library, Special Collections.]

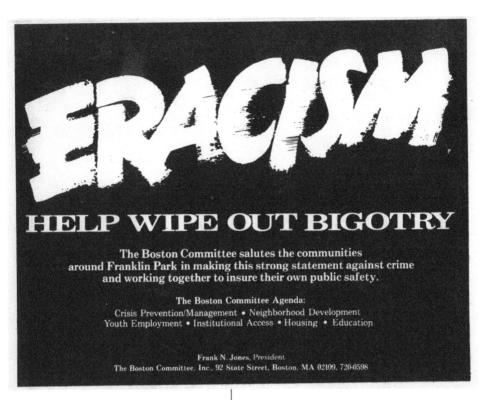

ERACISM

HELP WIPE OUT BIGOTRY

The Boston Committee salutes the communities
around Franklin Park in making this strong statement against crime
and working together to insure their own public safety.

The Boston Committee Agenda:
Crisis Prevention/Management • Neighborhood Development
Youth Employment • Institutional Access • Housing • Education

Frank N. Jones, President
The Boston Committee, Inc., 92 State Street, Boston, MA 02109, 720-0598

Bay State Banner supplement
July 1983
[Kay Bourne Archives at Emerson College:
Iwasaki Library, Special Collections.]

Concert ad
August 1980
[David Bieber Archives]

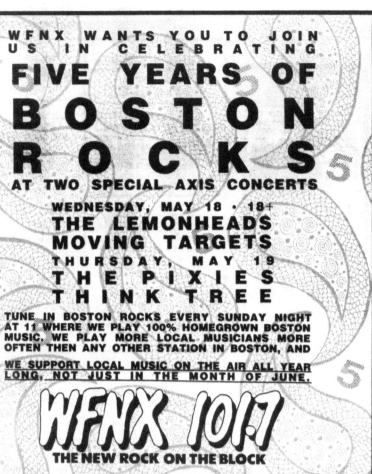

Boston Phoenix

May 13, 1988

[David Bieber Archives]

TONY ROSE

OF

SOLID PLATINUM RECORDS

IN ASSOCIATION WITH

CLUB 51

PRESENTS

"THE PARTY OF THE CENTURY"

FOR

Prince Charles

NEWLY SIGNED TO PAVILLION/CBS
FOR WORLDWIDE DISTRIBUTION

WHEN? SATURDAY, MAY 2, 1981 / 1:00a.m. - until......

WHERE? 51 THORNTON STREET, ROXBURY
(OFF WASHINGTON & CEDAR STREETS)

FEATURING:
OPEN BAR / BUFFET (UNTIL 3:00a.m.) / SLIDE SHOW /
LIVE ENTERTAINMENT / DISCO WITH THE SNAKE / LIVE
JAZZ / BILLIARDS, CHESS, BACKGAMMON / MOVIE SELEC-
TION - "RICHARD PRYOR LIVE IN CONCERT" / & MORE

MEET SPECIAL CELEBRITY GUESTS FROM NEW YORK & BOSTON

ADVANCED TICKETS ON SALE AT NUBIAN NOTIONS (DUDLEY)-$8:00
AT THE DOOR - $10:00

FOR INFORMATION, CALL TONY OR YVONNE :   442-2413

CELEBRATION TIME!! COME ON!!!!

Event / Party flyer

May 1981

[Kay Bourne Archives at Emerson College: Iwasaki Library,
Special Collections.]

The Noise

November 1988

[Author's collection]

Event flyer
February 1989
[Author's Collection]

BIG CITY

Mike Cassidy - Promoter

presents

ALL AGES!

BOOGIE DOWN PRODUCTIONS

featuring

KRS ONE
MS. MELODIE
D-NICE

and special guests
From **Toronto, Canada:** First Priority's Ragamuffin Rapper:

MICHIE MEE & D.J. L.A.LUV
T.D.S. MOB – GANGSTARR POSSE – KRISTY C.

Master Of Ceremonies: **KOOL D.J. ·RED ALERT**

THE STRAND

FRIDAY, FEBRUARY 17, 1989

Doors Open 7:30 pm   Showtime 8:00 pm
ALL AGES General Admission
$14.00 advance $16.00 at the door
Security will be provided by members of Muhammad's Mosque of Islam #11
Tickets available at Strawberries, Skippy White's, Mattapan Music, Nubian Notion, Spin City

543 Columbia Road , Upham's Corner, Dorchester   282-8000

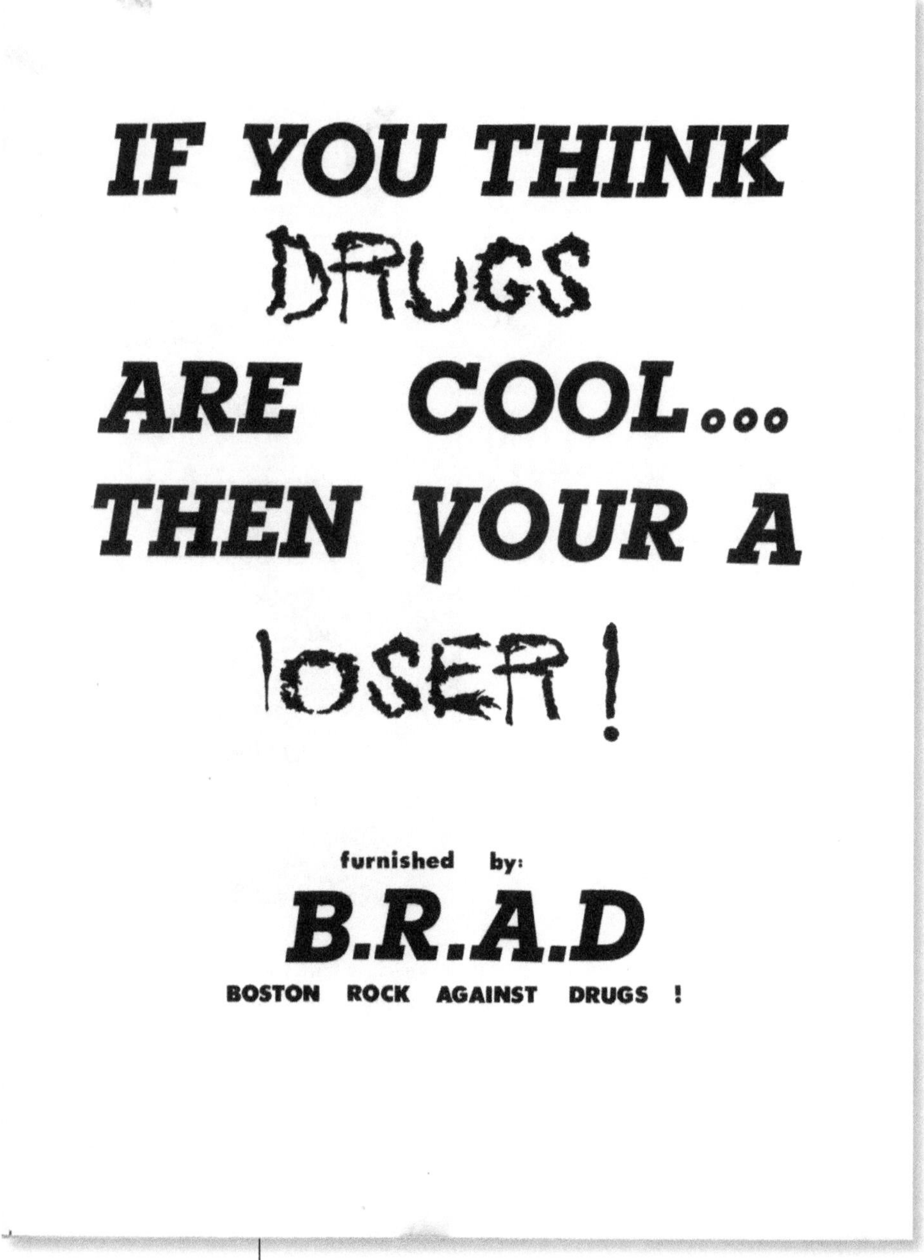

IF YOU THINK
DRUGS
ARE   COOL...
THEN YOUR A
lOSER !

furnished   by:
B.R.A.D
BOSTON   ROCK   AGAINST   DRUGS !

Boston Rock In [fanzine]
July 1987
[David Bieber Archives]

∂ISCO On Wheels

Franklin Field Skating Ring
Talbolt & Blue Hill Ave.

Open Daily from 12 noon to 11 p.m.

*SPECIAL DISCOUNT RATES FOR
CLUBS AND COMMUNITY AGENCIES*

LEARN TO SKATE

CALL TODAY   436-9210

KIDS LESSONS - SAT. 10:30 ADULT LESSONS - SUN. 10:30

(NO CHARGE)

The Sporting Life newspaper
May 19, 1977
[Kay Bourne Archives at Emerson College:
Iwasaki Library, Special Collections.]

1st ANNIVERSARY CELEBRATION OF

GEORGE MURRAY AND THE
ANGELIC CHOIR

OF BOSTON

BETHEL P. CHURCH

112 HUMBOLDT ST.   ★   **ROXBURY, MASS.**

FREE ADMISSION   **SUNDAY**   FREE ADMISSION

APRIL 21, 1968

1st SESSION — 3 P.M.

— SPECIAL GUESTS —

★ **CELESTIAL JRS.** OF BOSTON   ★
TABERNACLE CHOIR   ★   WALLACE SINGERS
★   RONNIE INGRAHAM CONCERT CHOIR   ★
WAY-OF-THE-CROSS CHOIR   ★   CRAYTON SINGERS
★   SIS. LESLEY CASEY and Her Fabulous "Cassetts"   ★

2nd SESSION — 8 P.M.

— SPECIAL GUESTS —

THE **ANGELIC CHOIR** CHURCH OF GOD IN CHRIST
EVANGELICAL GOSPEL SINGERS   ★   THE SINGING STARS
ALPHA & OMEGA SINGERS ★ MASS FELLOWSHIP CHOIR
★   SIS. GLADYS JAMES and Her TRUE LIGHTS   ★

M.C. SIS. D. BRACY   ★   PASTOR: REV. H. D. BELL

— BE ON TIME FOR A SEAT —

Concert poster

April 1968

[Kay Bourne Archives at Emerson College: Iwasaki Library, Special Collections.]

**Run-DMC is
The King of Rock
and Reads
The King of
Magazines**

photo by John Visser

the **BEAT!**

Yes, I want to subscribe. Here's my $15.00 for 26 issues (one year) of *The BEAT*. Please send my subscription and my free *BEAT*-Aid T-Shirt (Check color and size).

☐ Red   ☐ Yellow   ☐ Blue
☐ Small   ☐ Med.   ☐ Large   ☐ X-Large

NAME _____

ADDRESS _____

CITY_____ STATE _____ ZIP_____

Send check or money order to:
The *BEAT*, 8A Glenville Ave., Allston, MA 02134
782-ROCK

The Beat magazine

January 1986

[Author's collection]

Fenway Franks bring home plate to home plate.

Sometimes the best part of the game is the hot dogs that go with it.

You have to have a frank or two before you check out your scorecard.

And who takes a seventh inning stretch without a seventh inning snack?

Trouble was, you had to leave the taste behind when you left the park.

But now it's a whole new ballgame, because now you can take Colonial's Fenway beef Franks, the hot dog sold at Fenway Park, to your own home plate.

Pick up a package at your supermarket and rally the whole family.

Colonial

Red Sox program

1975

[Author's collection]

The Avatar

October 13, 1967

[David Bieber Archives]

Enjoy Great Chinese food?
Discover... Aku Aku

"Truly two of America's greatest Chinese restaurants and they're here in Boston and Cambridge"

**Ken Mayer
Entertainment Columnist
Herald American**

We deliver. Boston only. Orders of $10.00 or more within a 2 mile radius for $2 service charge.

Boston
390 Comm. Ave.
Phone: 536-0420

Cambridge
149 Alewife Brook Pkwy.
Phone: 491-5377

Free Garage Parking
4 p.m. – 3 a.m. daily
Happy Hour Mon.-Sat. 4-6

Ample Free Parking
11:30 a.m. – 2 a.m. daily
Luncheon served daily

Boston Magazine

December 1980

[David Bieber Archives]

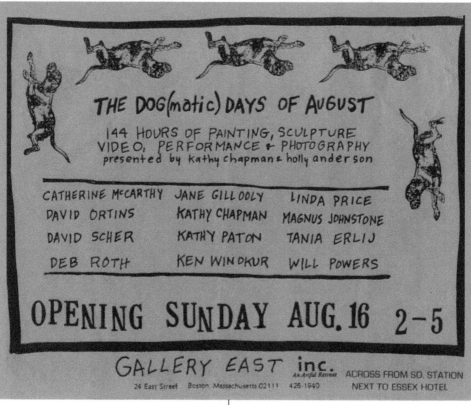

THE DOG(matic) DAYS OF AUGUST

144 HOURS OF PAINTING, SCULPTURE
VIDEO, PERFORMANCE & PHOTOGRAPHY
presented by kathy chapman & holly anderson

CATHERINE McCARTHY	JANE GILLOOLY	LINDA PRICE
DAVID ORTINS	KATHY CHAPMAN	MAGNUS JOHNSTONE
DAVID SCHER	KATHY PATON	TANIA ERLIJ
DEB ROTH	KEN WINOKUR	WILL POWERS

OPENING SUNDAY AUG. 16 2-5

GALLERY EAST inc.
An Artful Retreat
24 East Street   Boston, Massachusetts 02111   426-1940

ACROSS FROM SO. STATION
NEXT TO ESSEX HOTEL

Event flyer
August 1981
[Courtesy of Gallery East Productions]

Boston Magazine
October 1986
[David Bieber Archives]

THE BOUDOIR PORTRAIT

With Boudoir, your clothing is "as you
like it" a romantic negligee, or maybe a
favorite dress, for soft sensual portraits
photographed with sensitivity for that
someone special in your life. Truly an
unusual gift of love.

The STUDIO

101 PLEASANT STREET, MALDEN
OPEN TUESDAY-SATURDAY   321-0970

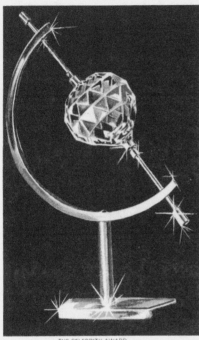

THE CELEBRITY AWARD

An H.C.M. Production

Boston's 3rd Annual
Celebrity Awards Show

Starring

Jonzun Crew • Rockers Revenge

- STARR/BLAZE • DARCEL SPEAR/EVERETT GIBSON
(Dancin' in the Street)
- PRINCE CHARLES
- SLYCK
- ELECTRIC POWER BAND
- KENRICK HAYNES
- PRESSURE DROP
- T WEST
- HYPERTENSION
- YVETTE CASON

also

Heartbeat • Larry Wedgeworth • Dr. Funkinchain & East Coast Funkateers • Lamont Swinson • Nuclear Rhythm Section • Bridget Tillet & Hakin Shariff Ensemble • Gold 24 Karat • Diane Stevens/The Bill Mackey Dance Theater • Mt. Pleasant Way Theater • Wheels • Fashion Shows by Therez/Lady Di/Immonnie Tafari • Ahteebah • Lacarr • Thomas Henry & Prudance • Hair Show by Charlene • Ethelite & Punks • Pulsarr featuring Robert Lovejoy • Starjamer, The Boston Rappers, Layzar • Kathy Brown • Loman "McClinton".

Master of Ceremonies
STEVE CRUMBLEY (WILD)
James A. Lewis, III — Elliot Francis

Friday, Oct. 15 — 7:00 p.m.

JOHN HANCOCK AUDITORIUM
180 Berkeley St., Boston, Mass.

Tickets Available At:
Strawberries, Nubian Notions, Skippy White, Danny's His 'N' Hers, Charlene's, Samuels for Hair, Lloyd & Jim's Musique Shop,
TICKETS - $12.00   For Information - 421-2000 or 427-4110

Concert / Event flyer

October 1982

[Kay Bourne Archives at Emerson College:
Iwasaki Library, Special Collections.]

The Avatar
August 4, 1967
[David Bieber Archives]

Boston After Dark
November 1, 1967
[Author's Collection]

[December 1981]

[May 1988]

Mon 5/16   JAZZ
THE NEITHER/NORCHESTRA
w/ Eric & Robb's "Oink Vay"

Tues 5/17   ACOUSTIC ROCK
Helldoracle Productions
Presents: THE EELS & Guests

Wed 5/18   LATIN FOLK
FORTALEZA

Thu 5/19   REGGAE
LOOSE CABOOSE

Every Fri   GREEK MUSIC
Every Sat   ARABIC MUSIC
                                until 2 a.m.
Fri & Sat   BELLY DANCER
                        between 9:00/9:30

Entertainment from:
8:45 pm - 12:45 am Mon-Wed
8:45 - 1:45 am Thu-Sat
Cover charge $5 unless otherwise indicated

472 MASS AVE CAMBRIDGE 354-8238

Salem Evening News "Teen Scene"
edition

Oct 1, 1966

[David Bieber Archives]

Salem YMCA Senior High Canteen

Featuring the Best in Bands
On the North Shore
DANCING EVERY SATURDAY NIGHT
★   **OCTOBER DATES**   ★

● **Oct. 1st—The Shaggs**   ● **Oct. 8th—The Warlocks**
● **Oct. 15th—The Kandymen**   ● **Oct. 22nd—Your Choice**
● **Oct. 29th—The Monks**

Sign Up Now at the YMCA

Win A Free Spinal Tap

Be one of the first 25 people to call (617)851-5772
after 9:00 p.m. Thursday, April 12, say "I need a
Spinal Tap from Polydor Records" and

WIN
a Spinal Tap Soundtrack LP &
1 pair of tickets to
This is

Spinal Tap

Playing exclusively at the

NICKELODEON
606 Comm Ave Boston 424 1500

Now available on LP or cassette at all
Coop, Side One, Good Vibrations,
Discount Records, and Recordtown
locations.

polydor

PolyGram Records

Sweet Potato, Mass Music, April, 1984 — 23

Sweet Potato magazine

April 1984

[Author's Collection]

In Celebration of Jamaica's
20th Anniversary of Independence

EMPIRE INTERNATIONAL PROMOTIONS and TAMBRAN RECORDS
PRESENTS

BOSTON'S FIRST
REGGAE FESTIVAL
COMPETITION

SINGING — SOLOS and
★ GROUPS ★ DJ's
BANDS — TROPHIES
✷ CASH PRIZES ✷

SAT. AUG. 7 8:00 PM - UNTIL 2 am

BROMLEY HALL

10 LAMARTINE ST. — JAMAICA PLAIN
(OFF COLUMBUS AVE. — HEATH ST.)

Advance Ticket $7 At Door $10

Persons interested in participating in the Competition contact:
Empire International Promotions, P.O. Box 506, Dorchester, MA 02125 or
Tel. 825-0649. Tambran Records Tel. 536-3003

Event flyer

August 1982

[Kay Bourne Archives at Emerson College:
Iwasaki Library, Special Collections.]

Boston After Dark
May 2, 1972
[David Bieber Archives]

Boston After Dark
November 1, 1967
[Author's Collection]

are you an

Exceptional Gal?

We are seeking a bright, attractive young woman who has all the secretarial skills and the willingness to earn over $10,000 a year. She must be free to travel, work long and irregular hours, and have the ability to meet and persuade the general public.

If you think you would enjoy such a position, please telephone Mr. Clifford at 426-2590.

Out of respect to the

memory of

John Fitzgerald Kennedy

the late President

of the

United States of America

all Filene stores

will be closed tomorrow

Monday, November twenty-fifth

Filene's

Boston Advertiser newspaper
November 24, 1963
[Author's Collection]

NAKED i
cabaret

**666
Washington St.
Tel: 338-9110**

Totally Nude College Girl Strip Tease

No Cover
No Minimum

Continuous Shows
12:30 P.M.-2 A.M.

In the heart
of Boston's
Adult
Entertainment
Area

Rolling Boulder magazine
1977
[David Bieber Archives]

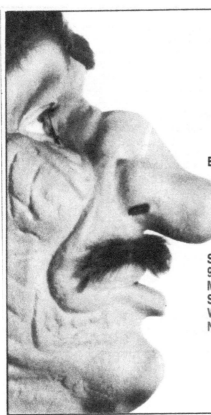

NOSE JOBS CHEAP!

But wait, there's more. Over a billion more bone-chilling faces for Halloween. All at Little Jack Horner's Joke Shop.

New Huge Headquarters:
50 Bromfield Street,
Boston, MA, Tel. 482-0219.

Specially Brewed Hours:
9 a.m. - 8 p.m.,
Mon. - Sat. until Halloween.
Sun. noon - 6 p.m. beginning Oct. 26.
We love cash. We take plastic.
No rubber checks.

Little Jack Horner's Joke Shop.

Boston Phoenix
October 28, 1986
[David Bieber Archives]

PLAN NOW!
MUTUAL UFO NETWORK
presents
12th Annual UFO Symposium At MIT (Cambridge)

Theme: UFO's The Hidden Evidence.
Sat. & Sun. July 25 & 26, 1981
For information, send a self-addressed stamped envelope to:
Ms. J. Thompson
60 Garden St.
Cambridge, MA, 02138
or call Joe & Diana Santangelo
617-944-2456

Real Paper
May 21, 1981
[David Bieber Archives]

The "Newbury St." Hair Design You Can Afford

▶ $12 **C**uts
▶ $20 **P**erms
▶ $10 **C**ellophanes
▶ $15 **H**ighlights
▶ $8 **C**uts
(with student I.D.)

YOU CAN'T BEAT THE SYSTEMS!

HAIR**S**YSTEMS
Samantha's place

297 Newbury St., Boston 266-1140
WALK IN SERVICE
Mon.-Fri. 10-8, Sat. 9-6
3 minute walk from Auditorium Ⓣ

Celebrity Awards event program
October 1982
[Kay Bourne Archives at Emerson College: Iwasaki Library, Special Collections.]

Boston Phoenix
September 10, 1985
[David Bieber Archives]

EDW. WILLIAM'S **Hair Focus**
UNISEX BEAUTY SALON

860 HARRISON AVE.
BOSTON, MASS. 02118
262-1400

Pardon Our
Appearance
We are remodeling
for our
Skin Care Salon

East West Journal
February 1974
[David Bieber Archives]

Henry Margu's cool capless wigs

Two marvelous wigs to give you two exciting new-
as-now looks. Both are capless, so they're not
heavy or hot. Both are more natural looking than
ever, because they're constructed from fine
Cordalon II fibers that rival the texture of your
own hair. Best of all, they're easy to care for,
retain their curl and are frizz-free. You'll want
the glamorous Petite Afro at only 12.00 and the
fluff-back Charmer at 13.00. Wig Salon,
Street floor, main store, D-205

BOSTON ONLY

Bay State Banner

March 9, 1973

[Kay Bourne Archives at Emerson College:
Iwasaki Library, Special Collections.]

Concert flyer

January 1982

[Courtesy of Gallery East Productions]

New England Scene

November 1968

[Kay Bourne Archives at Emerson College:
Iwasaki Library, Special Collections.]

WXKS

kiss-108

B O S T O N ' S   D I S C O   S T A T I O N S
FM 108   AM 1430

Boston Magazine
July 1979
[David Bieber Archives]

YOUR CONTRIBUTIONS WILL
KEEP ME IN THE GAME

THE JIMMY FUND • 44 BINNEY ST. •
KENMORE STATION • BOSTON, MA 02115

Red Sox program
1987
[Author's collection]

Boston Magazine
May 1985
[David Bieber Archives]

OYSTERS
Belong Behind Bars

UNION OYSTER HOUSE
41 Union Street, Boston, Mass. 227-2750

Boston After Dark
September 17, 1969
[David Bieber Archives]

Back Again....Better Than Ever!

THE
G - CLEFS

ATLANTIS
MUSIC PRODUCTIONS

P.O. Box 532
LAWRENCE, MASS. 01842

JERRY DiMAURO
TEL. (617   682-8677

Night Life magazine
November 1973
[David Bieber Archives]

Boston Rock magazine
August 1980
[David Bieber Archives]

SPit

10 PM till 1:37 AM
MUSIC BY WBCN's
OEDIPUS
Must be 20 years old

FINALLY BOSTON CAN DANCE
TO ROCK 'N' ROLL
EVERY FRIDAY AND SATURDAY
AND WEDNESDAY

DRESS: PUNK
13 LANSDOWNE STREET

BOSTON   262-2437

Win $100 for Best Dressed Couple ☆

IN CONCERT
FOR ALL AGES ☆

Win $100 for Best Dressed Couple

THE FLAMING STARR
MAURICE STARR

"Moving on Up"
"Come & See Me Some Time"
"'Bout Time I Funk You"
"If I Could Start All Over"

SPECIAL GUEST STAR M.C.
PRINCE CHARLES

"In the Streets"
"Passion"

PLUS
BOSTON'S OWN
JOHNSON BROS.

with the FUNK-E-FECT DANCERS

Sat., Nov. 1 — Carver Auditorium
80 Talbot Ave., Dorchester
Two Shows: 7-9 p.m. and 10 p.m.-Midnight

Admission: $7.50 Advance — $8.50 At Door

TICKETS AT: Skippy Whites, A Nubian Notion, Strawberries Records

A Boston International Record Production

Concert flyer
November 1980
[Kay Bourne Archives at Emerson College: Iwasaki Library, Special Collections.]

MELIAH KRAZE

THE
NORTH SHORE'S
KILLER HEAVY
METAL BAND
IS BACK!!

DO YOU KNOW WHERE YOUR CHILDREN ARE?

Preview Magazine

July 1984

[Author's collection]

Program front cover

June 1975

[Kay Bourne Archives at Emerson College: Iwasaki Library,
Special Collections.]

MITCH T-SHIRTS
100% COTTON
$6 ppd.-checks to T. MAX & COOKIE
specify size XS S M L XL
74 JAMAICA ST., JP, MA 02130

The Noise

September 1986

[Author's collection]

Celebrate!

BOSTON'S TRIBUTE to
DR. MARTIN LUTHER KING, JR.
AND
THE 350TH YEAR OF BLACK PRESENCE IN BOSTON

"Let The Holiday Unite Us"

Saturday, January 16 — Sunday, January 17

Program front cover

January 1988

[Kay Bourne Archives at Emerson College: Iwasaki Library, Special Collections.]

Broadside magazine

April 10, 1966

[Kay Bourne Archives at Emerson College:
Iwasaki Library, Special Collections.]

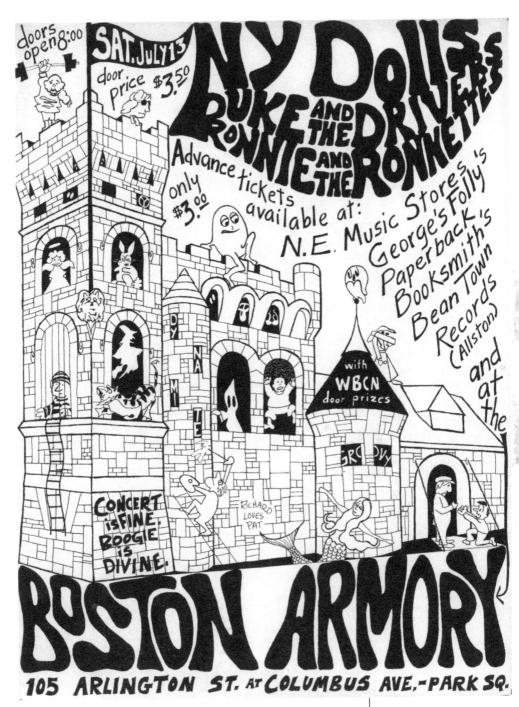

Concert flyer

July 1974

[David Bieber Archives]

Prince Charles who has just released his latest single "SKINTIGHT TINA" on Atlantic Records will make a special guest appearance at Collage Connection's Fifth Annual Designers Display Competition. He will be awarded H.C.M. Productions special Best of Boston Award which is presented to those persons who have achieved highly in the entertainment world.

In addition to his first album, "Gangwar" (originally produced on Solid Platinum Records), Charles has recorded four other albums, released on Greyhound Records, ROIR (Cassettes), MJS Records, and Virgin Records. Among them are the "Stone Killers" and "Combat Zone" albums. He also has twelve singles to his credit.

Prince Charles has toured extensively in the U.S., Canada and Europe, including such countries as: England, France, Belgium, Germany, Holland, Scotland, Sweden and Switzerland. He has also performed on tour with Jimmy Cliff, Rod Stewart, and Duran Duran in Madison Square Garden and other top U.S. concert halls. Prince Charles' latest single "SKINTIGHT TINA" is supported by a video, both produced by Prince Charles and Tony Rose / Solid Platinum Productions for Atlantic Records.

Designers Display Competition program

April 21, 1985

[Kay Bourne Archives at Emerson College: Iwasaki Library, Special Collections.]

Concert flyer

November 1988

[Courtesy of Diggers With Gratitude]

Concert flyer

February 1976

[David Bieber Archives]

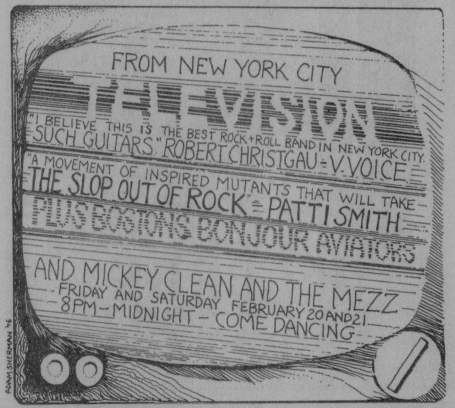

Roller Babe fanzine ad
1976
[David Bieber Archives]

Concert(s) flyer
1973
[David Bieber Archives]

UPTOWN IN THE PARK

White Stadium, Franklin Park, Boston

Vicki Lawrence

Phase I - July 7
Phase II - August 25
Phase III - September 2

If we can be of further assistance please call John Sdoucos at 617-262-6666.

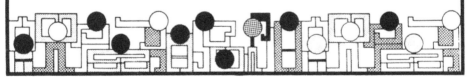

Masterworks, 10 Emerson Place, Suite 14e, Boston, Massachusetts 02114   617-262-6666

Program back cover

Photo by Vicki Lawrence

August 1974

[Kay Bourne Archives at Emerson College: Iwasaki Library,
Special Collections.]

ROCK TOUR JACKETS
A Great Gift Idea!

Duran Duran
Iron Maiden
Judas Priest
Motley Crue
The Police
ZZ Top

AND
MORE!

Available now at all locations!

AT STRAWBERRIES, THE TAPE NEVER
COSTS MORE THAN THE RECORD

IF YOU DIDN'T BUY YOUR MUSIC
AT STRAWBERRIES YOU
PROBABLY PAID TOO MUCH!

• BOSTON • Kenmore Square • Downtown Crossing • CAMBRIDGE • Harvard Square • 750 Memorial Drive • WATERTOWN • Watertown Mall •
SOMERVILLE • Twin City Plaza • MEDFORD • 25 Revere Beach Parkway • SAUGUS • Rte. 1 • FRAMINGHAM • Rte. 9 • DEDHAM • Dedham
Plaza • BURLINGTON • Crossroads Plaza • Burlington Village • CHELMSFORD • Drum Hill Road • WORCESTER • 10 Front Street •
SHREWSBURY • White City Shopping Center • AUBURN • 390 Southbridge Street • LEOMINSTER • Searstown Mall • PEMBROKE • North River
Plaza • PROVIDENCE, RI • 177 Union St • WARWICK, RI • Bald Hill Rd • MANCHESTER, NH • 1525 So. Willow St. • NASHUA, NH • Nashua
Mall • PORTSMOUTH, NH • 1981 Woodbury Ave at Gosling Street

Boston Rock #19

Boston Rock magazine

November 1984

[Author's Collection]

... **because it sounds better**

channel stereo four-channel stereo four-channel stereo four-channel stereo four-channel

WAAF 107.3 STEREOROCK

Night Life magazine
September 1973
[David Bieber Archives]

Bay State Banner

April 2, 1970

[Kay Bourne Archives at Emerson College: Iwasaki Library, Special Collections.]

Boston Phoenix
November 15, 1977
[David Bieber Archives]

IT'S HERE!
the new

WILD

"The Soul Sound" • Rhythm & Blues All Day

Dial 1090

CHUCK CALL
"WILD CHILD"

TONY
LEWIS

MARYE
HUNTER

JIMMY
"EARLY" BYRD

Boston Globe
April 3, 1967
[Author's collection]

PA, Disco & Recorded Music Systems for Theatres, Nightclubs & Musicians
SALES — SERVICE — RENTALS — LEASES — INSTALLATIONS
ALSO PORTABLE STAGE & CHAIR RENTALS
For FREE Estimates please write or call—

AUDIO TRANSPORT SYSTEMS

985 PLEASANT ST. BRIDGEWATER, MASS. [617] 697-6410

Night Time

November 1974

[David Bieber Archives]

Boston Rock magazine

December 1981 / January 1982

[Author's Collection]

Wash & Wear Cuts Without the Polyester

THE **NEW WAVE** HAIR SALON

1310 Boylston St. Boston, MA 02115
262-9131

The Sporting Life newspaper
May 19, 1977

[Kay Bourne Archives at Emerson College:
Iwasaki Library, Special Collections.]

The Real Paper
July 15, 1978

[David Bieber Archives]

10 Brookline St.
Cambridge, MA 02138
492-0082

Fri., April 8
DOGZILLA
SHE CRIED
LIMITED PARTNERSHIP
Sat., April 9
THE RAIN DOGS

BLAKE BABIES
INFORMATION
Sun., April 10
OONA'S
10th Year Anniversary Party
Proceeds to benefit Pine Street
Inn
4 p.m.
Tues., April 12
MYRIAD CREATURES
EVANGELISTS
SECTION 8
Wed., April 13
WUMB/91.9 FM presents
formerly of the Kingston Trio
T.T.'s is proud to present
JOHN STEWART
Thurs., Arpil 14
DHARMA BUMS
record release party
SALLY'S DREAM
BIG CLOCK
Fri., April 15
MIRACLE LEGION
MEN-N-VOLTS
THE NATIVES
Sat., April 16
RODS AND CONES
MAMBO X
WATER WORLD
Sun., April 17
a runner's diet . . . .
BARRENCE WHITFIELD
AND THE SAVAGES

PLATE O SHRIMP

491-7313

823 Main Street, Cambridge

Sun., Nov. 29
All Ages Admitted 4 p.m.
VOLTAGE
JACK DARLING
& SURPRISE GUEST

Weds., Dec. 2
NEW ROCK
SHOWCASE

Thurs., Dec. 3
THE RUNES
THE DEL FUEGOS
THE SCARED KIDS

Fri., Dec. 4
THE NEW MODELS
THE MYSTERY
DATES
PRIMITIVE
ROMANCE

Sat., Dec. 5
FUTURE DADS
THE M.I.A.'S

[November & December 1981]

[April 1988]

Tel.: 353-1865

Smiler
Haynes
Fashion

CUSTOM MADE CLOTHING
FOR MEN AND WOMEN
Also Ready to Wear Clothing
Accessories - Alterations - Repairs

56-A Gainsborough St.
Back Bay, Mass.

Get "A Stitch
to Fit"

The Sporting Life newspaper

May 19, 1977

[Kay Bourne Archives at Emerson College:
Iwasaki Library, Special Collections.]

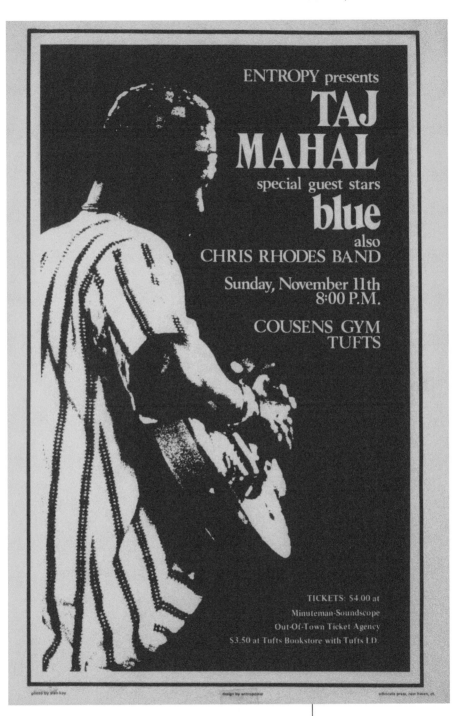

Concert poster

November 1973

[Courtesy of Reebee Garofalo]

Party invitation

November 16, 1985

[Kay Bourne Archives at Emerson College:
Iwasaki Library, Special Collections.]

JACK'S AUTOBODY & PAINT

IN OUR 3rd YEAR AS GREATER BOSTON'S FIRST GAY
OWNED, STAFFED & OPERATED BODY SHOP

OFFERING:
- Small Shop Personalization
- Completed on Chassis Restoration
- Return of Damaged Parts
- Late Model Rental Availability
- On Staff Licensed Appraiser
- Free Follow-Up Service

SPECIALIZING IN:
- Custom Painting
- Euro-Sport Look
- Classic & Antique Cars
- Japanese, German &
  Scandinavian Finishes

ONE WILLOW AVENUE   HYDE PARK   364-6481
T Stop Within 100ft   9 · 6 Monday · Friday

*Guide To The Gay
Northeast*

November 1987

[Author's Collection]

Boston Rock magazine

August 1980

[Author's Collection]

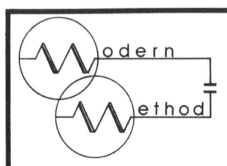

**odern
ethod**

**Coming soon on
Modern Method Records:**

Bound and Gagged 12" EP

**"No Surfin' in Dorchester Bay"
by Rich Parsons**

**Rerelease of "Heartbreaker"
by Thrills**

**"Italy's Underground Economy"
by The Uncommitted**

Modern Method Records
268 Newbury St.
Boston, MA 02116

Stuff Magazine
October 1986
[David Bieber Archives]

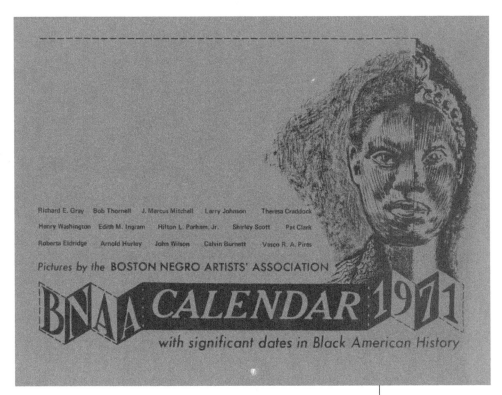

Calendar front cover

1971

[Kay Bourne Archives at Emerson College: Iwasaki Library, Special Collections.]

Before Television magazine
September 1988
[Author's collection]

GG Allin & The Scumfucs
DRINK, FIGHT & FUCK
EP NOW AVAILABLE

Buy It! Request It!
Die For It!
at Newbury Comics

Boston Rock magazine
August 1983
[Author's Collection]

PARASITES!
FASCISTS!
MORAL-BARBARIANS!

I WANT YOU
TO JOIN
THE NEW LEFT

WANT TO SAY YOU'RE FOR FREE SPEECH-
  WHILE SHOUTING DOWN OPPOSITION SPEAKERS?

WANT TO CALL YOURSELF AN INDIVIDUALIST-
  WHILE ADVOCATING SOCIALIST SLAVERY?

WANT TO PRETEND YOU'RE AN INTELLECTUAL-
  WHILE ACTING LIKE A MENTAL PATIENT?

THEN JOIN OUR ANTI-LIFE AXIS!

Sponsored by the people who think the New Left is SDS
(the SAME DAMN SH-T!)

 NEW RIGHT COALITION
330 Dartmouth Street
Boston. Mass. 02116

Boston University News
October 21, 1971
[David Bieber Archives]

RAMONES

TALKING HEADS

Special guest star from England:

EDDIE AND THE HOT RODS

Produced in association with **WBCN**

November 18   8 P.M.   Orpheum Theatre   All tickets: $4.50

Returns for Lynyrd Skynyrd Nov. 19 concert at Boston Garden will be available at point of purchase.

Tickets available at box office, Ticketron, Out-of-Town, and Strawberries.

Boston Phoenix
November 15, 1977
[David Bieber Archives]

The Guide To Gay New England

May 1986

[Author's Collection]

The Blackbyrds

at

TOGETHER

(formerly The Sugar Shack)

**110 Boylston St.
Boston, MA
426-0086**

**Thursday,
Friday,
Saturday,
& Sunday**

January 29 through February 1

2 Shows Nightly

**Tickets only available
at the Door.**

Another JJ Jam Production

Concert flyer

January 1976

[Kay Bourne Archives at Emerson College: Iwasaki
Library, Special Collections.]

Event poster

August 1984

[Courtesy of Reebee Garofalo and UMass Boston: Massachusetts Rock
Against Racism records, University Archives & Special Collections.]

[October & November 1984]

JOHNNY D's
Sound & Spirits
The Allston Alternative
85 Harvard Ave., Allston
254-9629

SAT. OCT. 27
**Odds, Moose &
Mud Bugs**

HALLOWEEN NIGHT
THE F.U.'s
plus (from NY)
**The Honeymoon Killers
and Sorry**

Thur. Nov. 1
**O-Positive
Sons of Sappho**

Sat. Nov. 3
**Volcano Suns
Christmas**

Wed. Nov. 7
**Wandells
Blaros**

Thur. Nov. 8
**Drezniak
Most Experts**

For Booking info Call 254-9629
Wed., Thur. & Sat. — 8:30-10:00

Johnny D's

Fri., May 13
BLUES YOU CAN USE

Sat., May 14
**JACK SMITH AND THE
ROCKABILLY PLANETS**

Sun., May 15
**BACK BREAKER BLUES
BLUE FEVER**

Wed., May 18
RODS AND CONES

TOO MUCH FUN

Thurs., May 19
BIM SKALA BIM

Fri., May 20
Cajun Dance Party
BOOGALOO SWAMIS

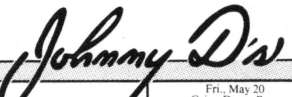

Sat., May 21
RONNIE EARL
(Ex Roomful of Blues)
JERRY PORTNOY
(Ex Muddy Waters)
& THE BROADCASTERS

Sun., May 22
EIGHT TO THE BAR

Coming:
Wed., May 25	**ROGER MILLER**
Thurs., May 26	**DUMPTRUCK**
Fri., May 27	**TREAT HER RIGHT**
with TOM PRINCIPATO
Sat., May 28	**URBAN BLIGHT**
Sun., May 29	**POUSETTE-DART
BAND**

[May 1988]

SEATING FOR 200   ON THE Ⓣ RED LINE
17 HOLLAND ST, DAVIS SQ. SOMERVILLE
776-9667

Attractions for College Concerts

Willie Alexander
and the Boom Boom Band

MCA RECORDS

Willie Alexander

Live, Willie Alexander and the Boom Boom Band is primal, spontaneous off-the-wall rock at its rawest and most original. Imagine a cramped, smoke-filled Boston snake pit mistakenly named the Paradise. The Boom Boom Band is playing a jagged, hard-edged firestorm of unrelenting rock while the maestro is staggering around the stage like a madman. Willie is talking/stuttering/singing/mumbling a wild ode; with a sly grin he grabs the mike stand and slowly sinks to the floor where he collapses into a crouch. The band lurches forward towards a photofinish of sound, the crowd is screaming their heads off, and Willie's sly grin still remains. Just tell them Willie Boy is here.

TROUSER PRESS/April 1978

AMERICA'S FASTEST GROWING FULL SERVICE AGENCY!

CALL TODAY FOR DATES & PRICES ON YOUR FAVORITE ARTISTS!

A&M RECORDS

In this time of fad, fashion and classification, a band called Dirty Angels just could be a punk band if one didn't take the time to check out the music behind the name. But with one listen it's obvious that Dirty Angels is a powerful and sensitive, gutsy and intelligent rock 'n' roll band.

the Energetics

showcasing
NEW ENGLAND

necaa

and many more local and national attractions...

AVAILABLE FROM THE FINEST COMPANY WITH THE FRIENDLIEST SERVICE...

DME

ONE SUCCESSFUL SHOW AFTER ANOTHER...
P.O. Box 362   Waltham   Mass. 02154   (617) 891-9365
666 Fifth Ave 12th floor New York 10019 (212) 246-4510

*Free expert assistance in planning, promoting and operating your concert

What's New magazine

October 1978

[David Bieber Archives]

[June & July 1987]

the PENALTY BOX Upstairs

ACROSS FROM BOSTON GARDEN

CAUSEWAY ST. NORTH STATION

WED JUNE 17
PLAY ETHICS
THE PHILTERS

SAT JUNE 20
EAST OF EDEN

THURS JUNE 18
THE GREENHEADS
DOGZILLA

THURS JUNE 25
ANESTHESIA SCREAM

FRI JUNE 19
THE HENDERSONS
COOL McCOOL
HIP CIVILIANS

MOVIE SUN JUNE 28
LAST HOUSE ON THE LEFT
GOREHOUNDS

FUNCTION ROOM & BAND BOOKING INFO CALL CHET 523-9160

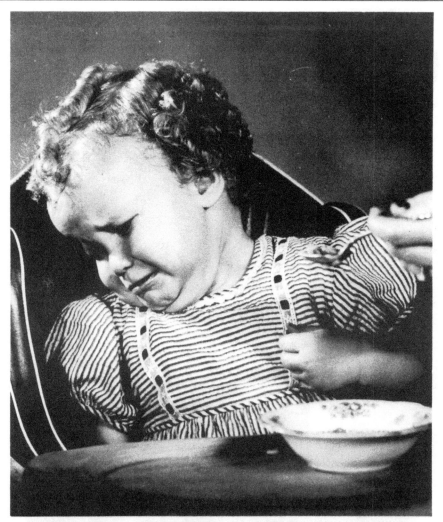

HOW DO YOU FEEL ABOUT HEARING THE SAME SONGS OVER AND OVER?

A lot of fans are fed up with radio stations playing good songs into the ground. They're tired of the new getting old too fast. That's why they're turing to WFNX 101.7 FM. We don't overplay the same paltry percentage of pop. We dish out more new music by more new artists than any other station. And if you want the best arts and entertainment coverage, then you want 101.7. Treat yourself to taste of WFNX. You'll never have to turn away again.

© Boston Phoenix Radio

101.7 FM WFNX
ROCK THE BOAT RADIO

Boston Phoenix
September 10, 1985
[David Bieber Archives]

Radio show flyer

1987

[UMass Boston: Massachusetts Hip-Hop Archive,
University Archives & Special Collections.]

Bay State Banner

February 8, 1973

[Kay Bourne Archives
at Emerson College:
Iwasaki Library, Special
Collections.]

journey back to
OLDE BOſTON

Where hospitality and fine dining
are a tradition

LOCKE-OBER CAFÉ
EST.—1875
3-4 WINTER PLACE
BOSTON
617-542-1340

Closed Sundays and Holidays

Boston Magazine

July 1979

[David Bieber Archives]

Event flyer

January 1988

[David Bieber Archives]

Your presence is requested at the most dazzling affair of the year.
THE NOISE, GREEN STREET & BIG WOW present

The 2nd annual   SUNDAY JANUARY 17, 8:30 pm

MAXIE AWARDS
GREEN STREET STATION
131 GREEN ST.   J.P.

The Masters of Ceremonies: The Band: Goo   522-0792
Patrick McGrath & Billy Ruane   The Hostess: Lucy Knight

The Presenters:

Mark V.   Lou Giordano
Eric Van   Wes Eichenwald
Charles White Bill Tupper
Tracey White   Jennifer Cares

Bill Abbate	Xanna Don't	Erik Lindgren	Doug Mellen	Oedipus	Albert O.	Mark Flynn
Willie Alexander	Ted Drozdowski	Joanie Lindstrom	Mark Melocarro	Mickey O'Halloran	A.J. Wachtel	Paul Robicheau
Jon Bernhardt	Kris Fell	Kathei Logue	Lois McGee	Julie Romandetta	Captain P.J.	
Bonnie Bouley	David Green	Tristram Lozaw	Brett Milano	James Ryan	Curtis	
Lilli Dennison	Bob Hamilton	David Mars	Su Miller	Debbie Shane	Steve Barry	NO COVER
Francis DiMenno	Tom Johnston	Jeff Marshall	Danny Mydlack	Shred		

HOT DOGS!

The box breaks.

The dirt flies. And in seconds eight of man's best friends merge into one powerful mass.

Lunging forward, reaching out, grabbing for that extra inch that puts one at the head of the pack.

You're at the rail.

One of a thousand screaming faces.

Trying to catch a glimpse of your dog, in amongst the multi-colored blankets and numbers, pounding past you at nearly 40 miles an hour.

The first race is over and you've gotten a taste of greyhound racing at its best.

Maybe even a taste of winning.

You've been up close, shoulder to shoulder with the railbirds, now sit back and experience greyhound racing from the inside.

Elegant dining and a superb trackside view are yours to enjoy in our clubhouse restaurant, while all hell breaks loose on the track just thirty feet away.

Wonderland. In Revere. First Race at 8.

Red Sox Yearbook

1981

[Author's Collection]

RONDAR
Magician,
Ventriloquist
& Master-of-
Ceremonies.
For parties,
banquets & cabarets. Twenty-four
hour service. 617 445-8960.

Night Life magazine
September 1973
[David Bieber Archives]

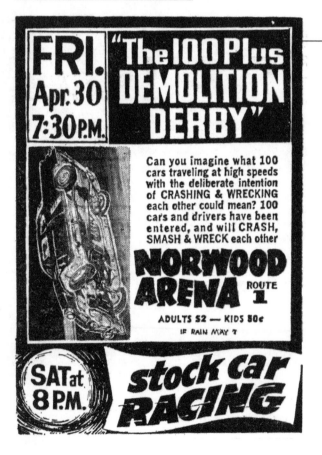

FRI. Apr. 30 7:30 P.M.

"The 100 Plus DEMOLITION DERBY"

Boston Record American
April 30, 1965
[Author's Collection]

Can you imagine what 100 cars traveling at high speeds with the deliberate intention of CRASHING & WRECKING each other could mean? 100 cars and drivers have been entered, and will CRASH, SMASH & WRECK each other

NORWOOD ARENA ROUTE 1

ADULTS $2 — KIDS 50¢
IF RAIN MAY 7

SAT at 8 P.M. stock car RACING

Being the adventures of a young man whose principal interests are rape, ultra-violence and Beethoven.

STARRING
MALCOM MC DOWELL . PATRICK MAGEE . ADRIENNE CORRI

Nebula magazine

January 1972

[David Bieber Archives]

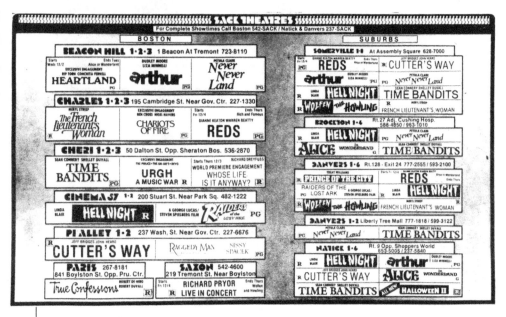

[December 1981]

Boston Phoenix
May 13, 1988
[David Bieber Archives]

Tuesday - Beyond Mud Wrestling
FEMALE JELLO WRESTLING
any girl is eligible

$50.00 for the winner each match
$25.00 for the loser each match

75¢ Domestic Bottled Beer
$1.00 Bar Drinks
8pm - 2am

Which jiggles more? The ring or the contestants?

The jiggles aren't just in the jello

Monday *Beat Inflation*
50¢ Bud drafts
75¢ domestic bottled beer
$1.00 mixed drinks
No Cover

Band — PHD
Fri. & Sat., December 4 & 5, 1981

the ARK
835 Beacon St.
247-9548

Boston Phoenix
December 1, 1981
[David Bieber Archives]

Boston After Dark

October 1, 1969

[David Bieber Archives]

CLUB 47, INC.

FEBRUARY 1965

SUNDAY	MONDAY	TUESDAY	WEDNESDAY	THURSDAY	FRIDAY	SATURDAY
1 P.M.—8 P.M. WHRB LIVE FOLK ORGY **1**	TOM RUSH	JIM KWESKIN **2**	IMAGE THEATRE WORKSHOP "THE RESERVATION" **3**	ALICE STEWART **4**	LES DANIELS AND SPIKE'S GROUP **5**	THE PICKABILLIES **6**
HOOTENANNY WITH MacSORLEY **7**	TOM RUSH **8**	CHARLES RIVER VALLEY BOYS **9**	IMAGE THEATRE WORKSHOP "THE RESERVATION" **10**	RICHARD & MIMI FARINA **11**	TONY & IRENE SALETAN **12**	JERRY CORBITT AND RAY PONG **13**
HOOTENANNY WITH R. L. JONES **14**	TOM RUSH **15**	JIM ROONEY AND BOB SIGGINS **16**	IMAGE THEATRE WORKSHOP "THE RESERVATION" **17**	CHARLES RIVER VALLEY BOYS **18**	SPIKE'S GROUP AND MacSORLEY **19**	R. L. JONES AND DERFK LAMB **20**
HOOTENANNY WITH BOB SIGGINS **21**	SQUARE DANCE WITH DUDLEY BRIGGS **22**	GEOFF MULDAUR AND MITCH GREENHILL **23**	IMAGE THEATRE WORKSHOP "THE RESERVATION" **24**	CAROLYN HESTER **25**	CAROLYN HESTER **26**	KEITH AND ROONEY **27**

Concert listings flyer

February 1965

[David Bieber Archives]

Boston Rock magazine

December 1981 / January 1982

[Author's Collection]

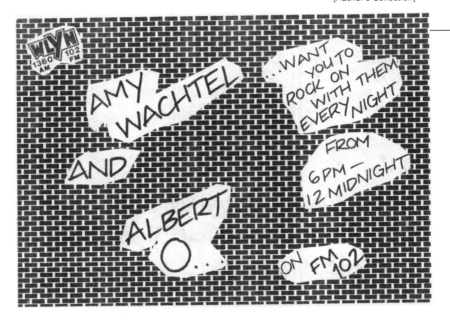

[September 1985]

God Guide fanzine

1982

[Wayne Valdez Archives]

The National Center of Afro-American Artists

invites you to

celebrate!

The Black Experience
June 11, 1971

at a

RECEPTION-EXHIBITION for Elma Lewis and Staff
Sponsored by the Friends of the National Center of Afro-American Artists
CITY HALL, BOSTON

then at the
American Première

of

KONGI'S HARVEST
written by WOLE SOYINKA
Filmed and Directed

by

OSSIE DAVIS
at Music Hall, Boston

finally

A Gala Revue and Party
at the
ELMA LEWIS SCHOOL OF FINE ARTS

Event flyer

June 11, 1971

[Kay Bourne Archives at Emerson College: Iwasaki
Library, Special Collections.]

Concert flyer
September 1973
[David Bieber Archives]

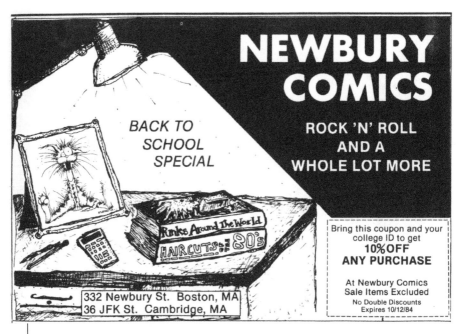

Boston Rock magazine

September 1984

[Author's Collection]

Real Paper

December 27, 1972

[David Bieber Archives]

OVER ALL THE WORLD, AND THROUGH ALL TIME
THERE ARE ONLY A FEW HUNDRED REAL BOOKS.
THE REST-DILUTIONS, DISTORTIONS, REPETITIONS
—LIKE MIRRORS IN A FUN HOUSE.
FROM 250,000 BOOKS IN PRINT WE'VE PICKED 1500.
SHAKESPEARE, SOME SAY, HAD SIX.

THE GRATEFUL UNION BOOKSTORE

1134 MASSACHUSETTS AVE. CAMBRIDGE, 02138 617-868-9637

10:30am to 7:00 pm monday thru saturday

· BUDDHISM · ISLAM · YOGA · TAOISM · ASTROLOGY · TAROT · ALCHEMY · CHRISTIAN MYSTICISM · PSYCHOLOGY · POETRY ·

Boston Phoenix

November 15, 1977

[David Bieber Archives]

The No Name Restaurant

*'Where the Fish Jump From the Ocean
Into the Frying Pan'*

Located on Boston's
Historic Fish Pier

15½ Fish Pier, Boston
338-7539
Open Monday-Thursday
10:30am-9:30pm
Friday-Saturday
11:00am-10:00pm
Never on Sunday

Real Paper
April 19, 1980
[David Bieber Archives]

Bay State Banner
June 6, 1974
[Kay Bourne Archives at Emerson College:
Iwasaki Library, Special Collections.]

Weddings

Windy-7 Studio

• *Portraits*   • *Functions*
• *Portfolios*   • *Baby Pictures*

6 Wellington Court
Dorchester, Mass.

Tel. 440-8765 427-9860

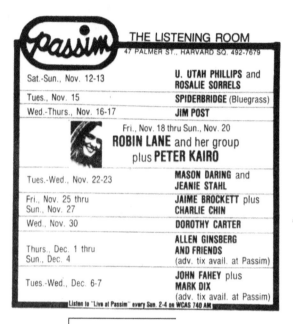

THE LISTENING ROOM

47 PALMER ST., HARVARD SQ. 492-7679

Sat.-Sun., Nov. 12-13	U. UTAH PHILLIPS and ROSALIE SORRELS
Tues., Nov. 15	SPIDERBRIDGE (Bluegrass)
Wed.-Thurs., Nov. 16-17	JIM POST
Fri., Nov. 18 thru Sun., Nov. 20	ROBIN LANE and her group plus PETER KAIRO
Tues.-Wed., Nov. 22-23	MASON DARING and JEANIE STAHL
Fri., Nov. 25 thru Sun., Nov. 27	JAIME BROCKETT plus CHARLIE CHIN
Wed., Nov. 30	DOROTHY CARTER
Thurs., Dec. 1 thru Sun., Dec. 4	ALLEN GINSBERG AND FRIENDS (adv. tix avail. at Passim)
Tues.-Wed., Dec. 6-7	JOHN FAHEY plus MARK DIX (adv. tix avail. at Passim)

Listen to "Live at Passim" every Sun. 2-4 on WCAS 740 AM

[November & December 1977]

McNASTY'S

88 Queensberry St.
(in the Fenway)
536-2509

Beginning Dec. 2
**WEDNESDAY
NIGHT
IS COLLEGE NIGHT**

**ROCK 'N' ROLL
DANCE PARTY**
featuring
Host DJ
PETER SIMON

Playing Your Requests
- No Cover -
75¢ Draft Pints - Drink
Specials

**Every Thursday
All Drinks 2 for 1**

Thursday, Dec. 3
the
**PAUL
RISHELL**
Band

Far City   Fri. & Sat.,
Dec. 4 & 5

**Don't miss
PETER SIMON**
Every Wednesday
**No cover - drink
specials**
Thursday - 2 for 1

Friday, Dec. 11

MIDNIGHT
TRAVELER

Saturday, Dec. 12
THE LINES

NO COST PARKING

[December 1981]

Summer in Paradise

967 Commonwealth Avenue, Boston

[July & August 1978]

THE CARS

June 30 - July 2 8:30 and 11 Tickets:
$5.50 June 30 and July 1 sold out
Tickets for July 2 still available

LAURA NYRO
BRYAN BOWERS

July 19 8:30 and 11 Tickets: $5.50
in advance, $6.50 day of show

MINK de VILLE
BILLY FALCON'S BURNING ROSE

July 20-22 8:30 and 11 Tickets:
$5.50 in advance, $6.50 day of show

KATE TAYLOR

July 5 8:30 Tickets: $3.50

SOUTHSIDE JOHNNY AND THE ASBURY JUKES

July 26 only

CARLENE CARTER AND THE RUMOUR

July 23-27, July 23-26: One show
only at 9 P.M. July 27: 2 shows, 8:30
and 11 Tickets: $7.50 in advance,
$8.50 day of show

ANTARES

July 30 8:30 Tickets: $3.50

DEAD BOYS

July 31 - August 1 8:30 Tickets:
$3.50 in advance, $4.50 day of show

LARRY CORYELL
LEE RITENOUR AND FRIENDSHIP

July 6 8:30 Tickets: $3.50 in
advance, $4.50 day of show

BRAND X

August 2 8:30 Tickets: $3.50

THE RAMONES
REAL KIDS

July 7 - 9 One show only: 9
P.M. Tickets: $4.50 in advance,
$5.50 day of show

BAIRD HERSEY AND THE YEAR OF THE EAR
ORACLE

July 10 8:30 Tickets: $3.50

JAMES COTTON BAND
ELOISE LAWS

August 3 8:30 Tickets: $3.50 in
advance, $4.50 day of show

MARTIN MULL

August 4-5 8:30 and 11 Tickets: $8.50

U.K.
RISER

July 11 8:30 Tickets $3.50

RICHIE FURAY

August 6 8:30 Tickets: $3.50 in
advance, $4.50 day of show

[May & June 1981]

The Paradise

"Boston's Best Concert Club"

967 Commonwealth Ave. Boston Tel. 254-2052 Positive ID required

Tonight, May 14	PERSUASIONS
May 15	JOAN JETT & THE BLACKHEARTS, The Orbits
Fri, May 16	TOM DICKIE & THE DESIRES
Sat, May 17	DOA, The Dark
Sun, May 19	BOW WOW WOW, New Models
May 20	INNER CIRCLE, Suade Cowboys
May 21	GARY "US" BONDS, Fast Fontaine
Fri, May 22	LEON REDBONE
Sat, May 23	THE PLASTICS, The Insect Surfers
Sun, May 24	THE COUNT'S ROCK & ROLL SPECTACULAR X
Fri, May 29	MIDNIGHT TRAVELLER, Wood 'n' Steel
Sat, May 30	TEARDROP EXPLODES, La Peste
June 2	ROBERT GORDON
June 3	JOE ELY
June 4	JUICE NEWTON
June 5	THE STRANGLERS, The Future Dads
June 6	KROKUS
June 12	PHOEBE SNOW

Salem Evening News "Teen Scene"
Oct 1, 1966
[David Bieber Archives]

ANOTHER **ALCON'S** FIRST

for guys and gals
doughboy leads
fashion parade

in CPO cloth
Navy -- Air Force Blue -- Dirty Camel
PRICE $14.95
COME IN AND SEE!

 Alcons Cove

A WHALE OF A SHOP

Open Wednesday, Thursday, Friday 'til 9 P.M.
COR. CABOT & WASHINGTON STS., BEVERLY

Heads-Up
Boutique

531-537 BROADWAY (RT. 28)
LAWRENCE. MA 682-1632

SATIN
SPARKLE
GLITTER
HIGHEST IN
NEW YORK &
WEST COAST
FASHIONS
Personal Checks Accepted

Specializing in stage and club attire.
Whether it be hard rock or a dressy
show, we have the styles for your band.

ROCK CLOTHES
STAGE CLOTHES
CLUB CLOTHES
FUN CLOTHES
We Have All The Clothes.

Group Discounts   Master Charge   Visa

*HOURS: TUES&FRI
10-8:30 PM
MON, WED, THURS, &
SAT 10-5:30 PM*

What's New magazine
October 1978
[David Bieber Archives]

TV program flyer

October 1971

[Kay Bourne Archives at Emerson College:
Iwasaki Library, Special Collections.]

Gay Community News
Dec 4, 1982
[Author's Collection]

The Avatar
June 9, 1967
[David Bieber Archives]

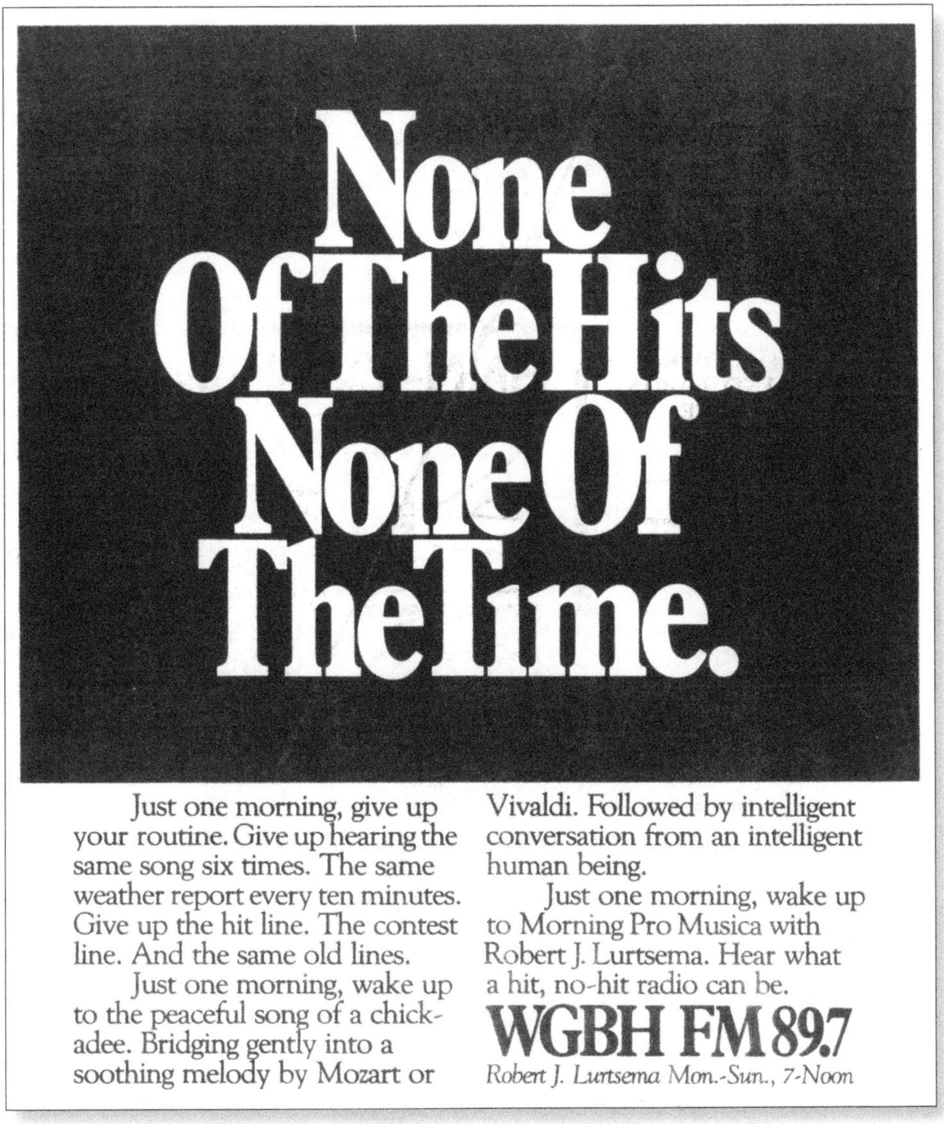

None Of The Hits None Of The Time.

Just one morning, give up your routine. Give up hearing the same song six times. The same weather report every ten minutes. Give up the hit line. The contest line. And the same old lines.

Just one morning, wake up to the peaceful song of a chickadee. Bridging gently into a soothing melody by Mozart or Vivaldi. Followed by intelligent conversation from an intelligent human being.

Just one morning, wake up to Morning Pro Musica with Robert J. Lurtsema. Hear what a hit, no-hit radio can be.

WGBH FM 89.7

Robert J. Lurtsema Mon.-Sun., 7-Noon

Boston Phoenix

May 13, 1988

[David Bieber Archives]

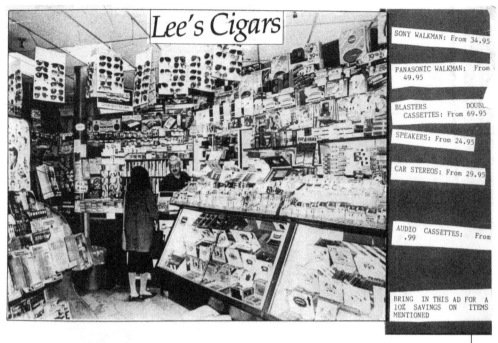

Lee's Cigars

SONY WALKMAN: From 34.95

PANASONIC WALKMAN: From 49.95

BLASTERS   DOUBL.
CASSETTES: From 69.95

SPEAKERS: From 24.95

CAR STEREOS: From 29.95

AUDIO CASSETTES: From
.99

BRING IN THIS AD FOR A
10% SAVINGS ON   ITEMS
MENTIONED

Street Magazine
1986
[Author's Collection]

SPIN CITY RECORD STORE
74 WARREN ST.
ROXBURY MA 02119

SPIN CITY RECORDS HAS BEEN VOTED
THE**BEST**
INDEPENDENT RECORD STORE IN BOSTON
The N.E.D.J. Assoc. and The Progressive Platter Magazine
Spin City's Guarantee of Satisfaction!!!
BEST PRICES IN TOWN / NEWEST RECORDS FIRST
LARGEST SELECTION OF R & B LP'S

*"We stimulate the mind, body and soul
with music that touches your heart."*

*Mass. Association
of Minority Law
Enforcement
Officers banquet
program ad*
October 1984
[Kay Bourne Archives
at Emerson College:
Iwasaki Library, Special
Collections.]

B̄LACK WEEKLY
NEW ENGLAND

"We Know New England —
We'd Like To Get To Know You"

**25 Huntington Ave., Suite 408
Boston, MA 02116
617-267-1377, 267-1379**

Celebrity Awards Program ad

October 1980

[Kay Bourne Archives at Emerson College:
Iwasaki Library, Special Collections.]

OFFICERS

President.................   Kenneth Ingraham
Vice President............   Barbara Harris
Secretary.................   Linda C. Buck
Treasurer.................   Elaine Wilson
Librarian.................   Ramona Paige
Asst. Librarian...........   Kenneth Robinson
Keeper of the Robes.......   Cecilia Baker

DIRECTOR

Hubert Walters

CO-DIRECTORS

Kathy Gatson
Clarence Hayes
Dardenella Robinson

Voices of a thousand!

For further information, write:
      The Kuumba Singers
      Harvard-Radcliffe Afro-American
                              Cultural Center

      20 Sacramento Street
      Cambridge, Massachusetts   02140

Group brochure front and back | 1973
[Kay Bourne Archives at Emerson College: Iwasaki Library, Special Collections.]

THE KUUMBA SINGERS

"We blacks sing...

Meaning to you,
a part of
Black US."

at WITS end!

1510 — the WITS end of your dial — sizzles with live coverage of every Red Sox game!

And on the 68 station Boston Red Sox Radio Network. Night games simulcast on WWEL-FM 108, and on WBET-AM 1460.

BROUGHT TO YOU BY: The Boston Globe, Budweiser Beer, Champion Spark Plugs, Your Nearby Coca-Cola Bottler, Colonial's Fenway Franks, New England Chrysler Plymouth Dealers, Delta Airlines, Sulfolk Franklin Savings Bank, The Yellow Pages, and Zayre Department Stores.

Photo courtesy of Jerry Buckley

WITS Radio 1510

Red Sox Yearbook

1978

[Author's Collection]

Real Paper
September 18, 1974
[Author's Collection]

LIVE FROM AFRICA ON BIG`
SCREEN CLOSED CIRCUIT TV

WORLD HEAVYWEIGHT CHAMPIONSHIP
DIRECT FROM KINSHASA, ZAIRE

NO RADIO   NO HOME TV

15 ROUNDS
TUESDAY
SEPTEMBER
24

GEORGE   MUHAMMAD
FOREMAN VS **ALI**

See the fight in color at Boston Garden, Boston Arena, Hynes Aud. - Boston, Music Hall Theatre, Lynn Ice Arena, Worcester Aud., Civic Center - Fitchburg, Cape Cod Coliseum, Rockingham Racetrack. In Maine, at Portland, Lewiston & Bangor.

Tickets now on sale at all Locations & All Ticketron Outlets.

Party / event invite
March 1985
[Kay Bourne Archives at Emerson College:
Iwasaki Library, Special Collections.]

Say Brother salutes
Allan Rohan Crite
on the occasion of his
75th birthday
Thursday, March 28, 1985
WGBH
125 Western Avenue
Boston, Massachusetts
8:00 p.m. to 10:00 p.m.
The party will be broadcast
that evening on Channel 2
After Five Attire
R.S.V.P. — 492-2777, ext. 2460

THE BOSTON KITE FESTIVAL

Kevin H. White
Mayor

Robert R. McCoy
Commissioner

Sat. May 14, 1983
Franklin Park

Sponsored by
Boston Parks
and Recreation

People
love our parks.

and

 Burger King

Franklin Park Festival '83

Event poster

May 1983

[Kay Bourne Archives at Emerson College: Iwasaki Library, Special Collections]

Fluid Dynamics
99 Mt. Auburn St.
Harvard Square
Cambridge, Mass.
661 1559

Hours:
Monday–Saturday 10–7
Thursday 10–9

Boston Phoenix
April 2, 1974
[David Bieber Archives]

Bay State Banner
April 4, 1974
[Kay Bourne Archives at Emerson College:
Iwasaki Library, Special Collections.]

JOIN US!!
at the FABULOUS FORTIES/SEXY SEVENTIES
BOOGIE-DOWN BIRTHDAY BENEFIT BASH !

For DANA C. CHANDLER, JR., (AKIN DURO)

at the
WILLIAM E. REED AUDITORIUM
(Prince Hall Masonic Temple)
24 Washington St., Grove Hall, Roxbury

FRIDAY, APRIL 5th....8 30 pm until!

featuring

WEBSTER LEWIS   **The RONALD INGRAHAM CONCERT CHOIR**

Hosted by

TOPPER "Say Brother" CAREW & BAND
and JAY CEE the D.J.(of 'The Ghetto" Fame)

DONATION $3.50 (at the door) -- $2.50 (w-Student ID)
All tickets at the door.

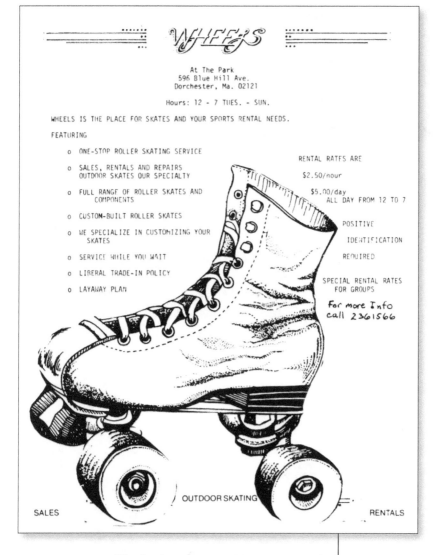

Elite Designers competition program ad

September 13, 1981

[Kay Bourne Archives at Emerson College: Iwasaki Library, Special Collections.]

First & Only
Boston Showing

BEHIND THE
GREEN DOOR

Starring

Marilyn Chambers

*"Do you remember the
Ivory Snow girl?"!*

pru cinema
903 BOYLSTON ST. ● 262-6200

Boston Phoenix
April 2, 1974
[David Bieber Archives]

Night Life magazine
April 1973
[David Bieber Archives]

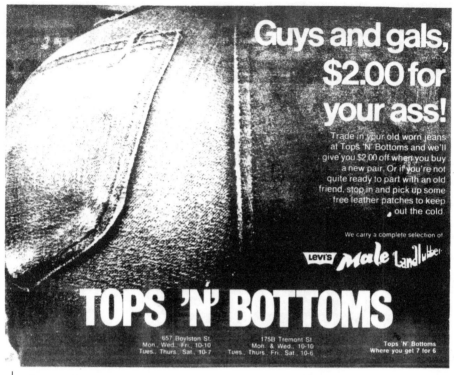

Boston University News
October 21, 1971
[David Bieber Archives]

East West Journal
February 1974
[David Bieber Archives]

Harvard Square is where it's at.

Over the basicbankerbroker barrier. Past the more boring boutiques. And into a whole new expression in menswear that transcends cultural gaps. With a Nashville cache of jeans, bells, flares, wide-cuffed, low-waisted, in country colors as well as neon lights. The softest, widest ties and scarves in the Western world. Enough imported jerseys and vests to fill up the Continental Shelf. Belts. Suits. And sheer shirts that show it like it is. Simon and Sons let it all hang out in Harvard Square. And Boylston Street, Charles Street, and South Shore Plaza. That's where it's at. And it's beautiful.

Simon & Sons

Boston, Cambridge, Braintree

Boston After Dark

October 1, 1969

[David Bieber Archives]

Boston Phoenix
September 10, 1985
[David Bieber Archives]

Boston Phoenix

July 4, 1978

[David Bieber Archives]

Nebula magazine

December 1971

[David Bieber Archives]

The Real Paper
May 29, 1974
[David Bieber Archives]

Cool, colorful clothing and accessories for girls' sizes 4– teen 14. Kicky. With a flair for fun. Funky. With a look you won't find everywhere else. That's Razz'ellez. And isn't that you?

Razz'ellez
201 Newbury Street
Boston   262-4646
Our other store–
Active Ingredients,
Sudbury   443-3178

Boston Magazine
August 1987
[David Bieber Archives]

*Designers Display Competition
program ad*

March 11 1983

[Kay Bourne Archives at Emerson College:
Iwasaki Library, Special Collections.]

here is a 2/23/78

banner

Exclusive...

DANCE...DANCE...DANCE!

Dance non-stop to the music of **STANTON DAVIS and the GHETTO MYSTICISM** and **DISCO** hits spun by WILD disc jockeys.

Shine with hundreds of Massachusetts' brightest stars at the new Cambridge Hyatt-Regency Ballroom on Saturday, March 4, from 9-1 a.m. And wear your finest.
Crash the winter hum drum with the biggest and baddest party this side of New York.
Only $10.00 admission (at the door), and this gets you a one-year subscription to the Bay State Banner.

Don't forget, Saturday, March 4 at the Hyatt-Regency in Cambridge.

Bay State Banner

February 23, 1978

[Kay Bourne Archives at Emerson College:
Iwasaki Library, Special Collections.]

Where It's At

*660 Beacon St.
in Kenmore Sq.*

April 8 - 10

**JOHN LEE HOOKER
& THE HALLUCINATIONS**

April 12 - 14

THE TOWEDS

April 15 - 17

**JERRY LEE LEWIS
& BAND**

dancing six nights a week

men - jackets & ties, please !
ladies - appropriate dress   **8 - 12**

*show- fri. & sat. 8:30 & 10:30
sun. 3:30 & 8:30*

*Broadside
magazine*

April 10, 1968

[Kay Bourne Archives
at Emerson College:
Iwasaki Library,
Special Collections.]

The Avatar

December 8, 1967

[David Bieber Archives]

**the
AQUARIAN AGE**

OCCULT & METAPHYSICAL
BOOKS & OBJECTS

astrology..tarot..kabalah
..palmistry..s.s.p...magic
..mysticism..psychedelics..
prophecy..color & sound..
hermetic science
..numerology....alchemy
astral projection.. i-ching

279 BROADWAY   CAMBRIDGE

Monday - Sunday
March 12-18

BRUCE
SPRINGSTEEN

✳

–March 20-25 –
Gram Parsons
with **Barry Tashian**

–March 26-April 1–
Tim Buckley

Oliver's
62 Brookline Ave
Boston

Boston Phoenix
March 13, 1973
[David Bieber Archives]

Boston Rock magazine
August 1980
[Author's Collection]

OUR SHIP HAS COME IN

The sound of hammers like the pounding of drums
The rhythm of saws and drills give the building a new life
Like a rhythm track the walls are put into place with care
*   and forethought*
a drum isolation area here, a vocal booth there, a spacious
*   control room,*
Three practice suites, and a couple of lounges for resting
*   and reflection.*
Our dream has become a reality; come record with us,
*   come practice with us,*
Come celebrate with us.

The new Euphoria recording and practice facility.

The New Euphoria Sound
Recording & Practice Facility
284-9707
90 Shirley Ave. Revere, MA

Boston's gone wild over

WILD
1090AM

Sign-On to 10AM: Sunny "Joe" White
10AM to 11AM: People's Platform
11AM to 2PM: Lark Logan
2PM to Sign-off: Eliot Francis

Nightfall magazine

September 1978

[David Bieber Archives]

Concert flyer

February 1983

[Courtesy of Peter Prescott]

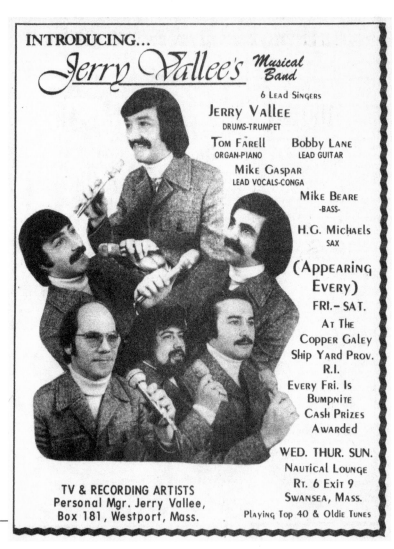

Night Life magazine
April 1975
[David Bieber Archives]

Lee® Rider Super Straight Leg

Cut lean for that clean, slim "authentic western" look. Wear them rolled up or tucked in your favorite boots. It features back pockets with compound curve stitching, front scoop pockets and Lee's famous branded logo patch on the waistband. In 100% Cotton Indigo dyed 14 ounce denim.

Authentic western styling makes this bell bottom jean distinctive. It features compound curve stitching on back pockets, scoop front pockets with watch pocket and Lee's famous leather patch on the waistband. Available in a variety of fabrics including 100% Cotton Indigo dyed denim and 84% Cotton, 16% Polyester 14 Wale Corduroy.

Lee® Rider Bell Bottom

Authentic western styling makes this bell bottom jean distinctive. It features compound curve stitching on back pockets, scoop front pockets with watch pocket and Lee's famous leather patch on the waistband. Available in a variety of fabrics including 100% Cotton Indigo dyed denim and 84% Cotton, 16% Polyester 14 Wale Corduroy.

Cut lean for that clean, slim "authentic western" look. Wear them rolled up or tucked in your favorite boots. It features back pockets with compound curve stitching, front scoop pockets and Lee's famous branded logo patch on the waistband. In 100% Cotton Indigo dyed 14 ounce denim.

slax & jeans
FACTORY OUTLET

21 Perkins Ave.
Brockton, Mass. 583-6054

249 No. Main St.
Randolph, Mass. 986-5420

227 Quincy Ave.
Quincy, Mass. 773-7285
(President Plaza)

Boston Phoenix
April 24, 1973
[David Bieber Archives]

KRACO AM/FM/MPX TAPE DECK
Reg. 99.88 Save $10
Now 89⁸⁸

Includes four speakers to surround you with music.

CAMBRIDGE ● DANVERS
DEDHAM ● SPRINGFIELD

LECHMERE
WHERE YOU POCKET THE DIFFERENCE

Boston Phoenix
November 15, 1977
[David Bieber Archives]

MOOD OF SPRING . . . WALKER'S STARTS THE ACTION WITH STYLE!

FRENCH SAILOR SHIRT

IS HITTING ALL THE HIGH NOTES
FOR GUYS AND GALS AT WALKER'S

We've taken the French Navy shirt . . . made it still better in a rugged cotton rib in 2 traditional colors — navy stripes and Breton red stripes on natural, unbleached background.

Sizes: small, medium, large, extra large.

6⁹⁵

"NAUTICAL" BELL BOTTOM JEANS
Navy • Breton Red • Scrubbed Denim

5⁹⁵

DUTCH BOY CAPS!

"Mod", "Fiddler", "Pussycat", "Arthur" — call it what you will. Wide wale corduroy in colors: burgundy, antelope, black, loden.

4⁹⁵ Sizes: small, medium, large, extra large.

YOU'RE ALWAYS A WINNER WITH

Walker's
THE STORE THAT SETS A TREND!

Open Wed. Evening till 8:15 PM

Walker's RIDING APPAREL, INC. 292 Boylston St., Boston (opposite Public Gardens) Tel. 267-0195

KREY'S DISC

in Boston	Northshore	Southshore
60 Boylston St. every day til 8:30	Northshore Plaza Peabody	Southshore Plaza Braintree
116 Bromfield St.	Northgate Plaza Revere	Westgate Plaza Brockton
623 Washington St.		

Bring in this ad for these prices

ANNOUNCING THE OPENING
OF OUR NEW PRUDENTIAL CENTER STORE.

TO CELEBRATE THE OPENING OF UPTOWN BOSTON'S MOST COMPLETE RECORD DEPARTMENT,

WE ARE OFFERING AN ADDITIONAL **10 %** ON OUR REGULAR DISCOUNTED PRICES

TO ALL OF OUR CUSTOMERS. FOR THE CONVENIENCE OF LATE SHOPPERS, THOSE WHO LIVE IN THE AREA, AND FOR THOSE OF OUR CUSTOMERS WHO FIND THE NEW STORE MORE CONVENIENT THAN OUR OTHER LOCATIONS, WE WILL CARRY A WIDE SELECTION OF TRADITIONAL AND MODERN JAZZ, CLASSICAL, POPULAR, AND A BROAD RANGE OF SELECTIONS FROM THE MAJOR RECORD CATALOGUES AVAILABLE IN THE UNITED STATES. WE WILL ALSO CARRY A COMPLETE LINE OF SHEET MUSIC, CLASSICAL AND FOLK GUITARS, HARMONICAS, AND ASSOCIATED ACCESSORIES.

OPEN EVERY EVENING EXCEPT SATURDAY UNTIL 9 PM

Broadside magazine

April 10, 1968

[Kay Bourne Archives at Emerson College:
Iwasaki Library, Special Collections.]

the spring orgy

WHRB's 38th semi-annual orgy period begins on May 4, 1972 with 24 hour a day special programming of classical, jazz, rock, folk, soul, R & B, C & W and various other things. For a free 40 page program guide to this spring orgy send your name and address and zip code to Orgy Director, WHRB, 45 Quincy Street, Cambridge 02138 or call 495-4818.

Cambridge Community Radio

whrb
95.3 fm stereo

*VVAW Winter Soldier Investigation, Apr. 24-28 at 12 Noon.

Boston After Dark

May 2, 1972

[David Bieber Archives]

every week more & more people are picking up their copy of BOSTON after dark

at

RICHDALE Milk and Food SUPERETTES
WHERE THE SHOPPING IS EASY
THERE'S ONE IN YOUR NEIGHBORHOOD

More than 65 stores open 7 days a week until 9:30 PM

For information on the nearest Richdale Superette that carries Boston After Dark please call 536-0363

whrb & the new music society present in concert

also appearing: "THING"

THE GARY BURTON QUARTET

featuring gary burton vibes
mick goodrich guitar
abe laboreal bass
harry blazer drums

Saturday, May 6th, 8 p.m.
Sanders Theatre ● Harvard University
tickets $2.00 at the door / the harvard coop / new directions

THE BEST HOUSE IN TOWN!

LULU WHITE

Jazz Supper Club
In Boston's South End

Creole American Cuisine
Willard Chandler, Chef

Tuesdays - Thursdays	**Fridays & Saturdays**
Name Jazz Attractions	*The Lulu White Jazz Dance Band*

Sunday Nights
Special Concerts

3 Appleton Street, Boston

for reservations call 423-3652

Red Sox Yearbook
1978
[Author's Collection]

BERTHA COOL
VINTAGE CLOTHING
528 COMM. AVE. BOSTON 247-4111
MON.- SAT. 11-6 (thursday until 8)

buy things here for spring

The Noise

April 1984

[David Bieber Archives]

Boston Magazine

December 1980

[David Bieber Archives]

WHERE'S BOSTON?

at

CAMBRIDGE WESTERN WEAR

1154 Mass. Ave. Cambridge
Mon-Sat 10-6, Thu. 'till 9PM
868-0959

IN YOUR EAR

739-1236

1236 COMM AVE

(Intersection of Harvard & Comm.)
Allston, MA 02134 739-1236
New and Used Albums, 45's and Cassettes
Bought, Sold & Traded

2 FOR 1 ADMISSION
ANYTIME!
SPINOFF
The Rollerskating Club
Corner of Ipswich and Lansdowne Sts.   Kenmore Square • Boston • 437-0000
Expires Jan 31 1985

say you saw it in the COMET

—JOHNNY D's—
—SOUNDS & SPIRITS—
—The Allston Alternative—
85 Harvard Ave. Allston
254-9629

Thurs., Nov. 1
O Positive
Sons of Sappho

Sat., Nov. 3
Volcano Suns
Christmas

Wed., Nov. 7
The Wandells
The Blaro's

Thurs., Nov. 8
Drezniak
Special Guests

Sat., Nov. 10
Classic Ruins
Band 19

Wed., Nov. 14
The Daughters
The Visigoths

Thurs., Nov. 15
Scruffy the Cat
Lifeboat

For booking info call night
of the Bands 8:30-10 p.m.
ask for RICK PAIGE

Kenmore Comet
newspaper
November 1984
[David Bieber Archives]

Boston After Dark
November 1, 1967
[Author's Collection]

UNICORN
COFFEE HOUSE
DAVE VAN RONK
and the HUDSON DUSTERS

Boston After Dark
October 1, 1969
[David Bieber Archives]

Congratulations and Best Wishes
For Your 14th Annual Awards Banquet

BLACK PROFESSIONAL FIREFIGHTERS
VULCAN SOCIETY of MASS., Inc.

P. O. BOX 269 - ROXBURY, MASSACHUSETTS 02119
Telephone (617) 436-0019

President, Robert L. Powell

Affiliations
International Association of Black Professional Firefighters
Life Member, N.A.A.C.P.

MATTAPAN BOARD OF TRADE, INC.

1624 BLUE HILL AVENUE, MATTAPAN, MASS. 02126
Telephone 296-0802

Celebrating 50 Years of Service to the Community

Stuart H. Rosenberg, *President*
Lenzer Evans, *Vice President*
Nick Nasson, *Treasurer*
Adelaide Freedman, *Secretary*
Rossetta Williams, *Corresponding Secy.*
Mort Tallen, *Chairman of the Board of Directors*

THE SQUARE
MATTAPAN SQUARE SHOPPING CENTER
"Gateway to Boston"

Massachusetts Association of Afro-American Police banquet program ad
October 1982
[Kay Bourne Archives at Emerson College: Iwasaki Library, Special Collections.]

Concert poster
October 1988
[Courtesy of Peter Prescott]

IN THESE TRYING TIMES....

GET YOUR WEEKLY DOSE OF P.M.A.*

WITH

CHOKE & KATIE THE KLEENING LADY

AND THE 'FASTER THAN YOU'

SHOW

P.M.A. ends "bunching and pulling" drudgery at your ironing board

i've got that attitude!

Bad Brains Rule!

SUNDAY EVENING
AT 7:30 BEFORE METROWAVE WITH CARMALITA

WERS-FM 88.9

SAN ANTONIO, Texas (UPI) — Punk rock performer Ozzie Osbourne was arrested Friday for urinating on the Alamo.

"My main goal in life is to use the White House steps as a public restroom," he said.

"If I had a kid, I wouldn't let him come to my show," he said.

ONLY IN THE BOSTON HERALD AMERICAN!

(not on the "faster than you" show!)

ALSO THE HARDCORE HOUR w/ DAVE SMALLEY, THURS. 9-9:15 on WZBC 90.3 XXX UNITED BOSTON RADIO!

* POSITIVE MENTAL ATTITUDE

Radio show flyer

1982

[Courtesy of Gallery East Productions]

Event program, front and back covers

October 1973

[Kay Bourne Archives at Emerson College:
Iwasaki Library, Special Collections.]

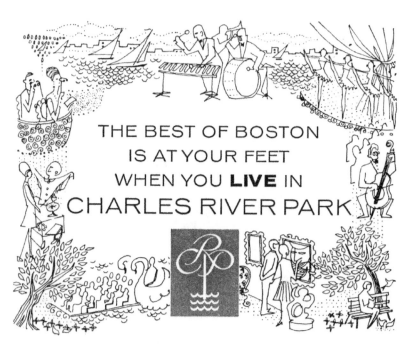

THE BEST OF BOSTON
IS AT YOUR FEET
WHEN YOU **LIVE** IN
CHARLES RIVER PARK

The Best Of The Old, The Best Of The New . . . you're just minutes from down-town . . . a short walk to work or pleasure • The Public Gardens • Newbury Street shops • Beacon Hill • Symphony Hall • The Hatch Shell • theaters • movies and restaurants • the Museum of Fine Arts • the Museum of Science • and the riverside sailing pavilion . . . all yours!

THE PRIVATE WORLD OF CHARLES RIVER PARK

Seclusion in the City . . . Boston's most luxuriously convenient apartments, set amid acres of private gardens, trees and lawns, overlooking the beautiful Charles River. Every apartment with individually controlled central air conditioning, huge terrace, large rooms, walk-in closets. Deluxe-equipped kitchen, including dis-posal, free gas. Parking and play areas. Every service, from casserole catering to maid service to wine cellar.

LEASE NOW while the apartment of your choice is available! Studio apart-ments from $125 to $160; 1-bedroom apartments from $155 to $225; 2-bedroom apartments from $258 to $330 (2 baths); 3-bedroom apartments from $282 to $425 (2 baths); 3-bedroom, 2½-bath duplex Town Houses from $365 to $385; 3-bedroom, 2-bath Town Houses with Garden from $390 to $425.

EXCLUSIVE RENTAL AGENT

Chamberlain *real estate*

60 Charles Street • CApitol 7-5520
Open Daily and Saturdays and Weekday Evenings

Colonial Theater program ad
August 1961
[Author's Collection]

Boston Record American
April 30, 1965
[Author's Collection]

SAVILLE ROW
CUSTOM CLOTHIERS

The entertainers tailors specializing in original designs of "on stage" clothing at a price that is competitive with your neighborhood mens shop.

We can creat any design in the fabric of your choice from the glitter look to the conservative lounge style.

Currently dressing noted sports personalities such as Boston Celtics JoJo White, John Havlicek, Paul Westphal, and Steve Kuberski . . . New England Patriots John Hannah, Tom Neville, Leon Gray, Ray Hamilton, and George Webster . . . as well as many performing groups as Mass Pike, Great Road, Mark 3, Image, and the Great Pretenders.

FOR ADDITIONAL INFORMATION:
617-321-2635 — **Herb Serpa**

Night Time magazine
January 1975
[David Bieber Archives]

Sweet Potato magazine
February 1982
[Author's collection]

Repair, Maintenance & Custom Servicing of:
● Guitar & Keyboard Electronics ● Instrument Amps ● PA Systems

AZTECH ELECTRONICS
40 Landsdowne St., Cambridge, MA 02139   876-4567

UPTOWN 965 HOSTS BENEFIT FOR ROSIE'S PLACE

Photography:
Chris
Pomiecko

SAFE
SEX CAN BE
GREAT!

You may not feel that safe sex is great. Or you may want to become safer but are finding it difficult.

GLCS is forming a 12-week group for gay and bisexual men who want to explore facts and feelings about sexual risk reduction. We think it is important to:
- separate fact from fiction, and distinguish "unsafe" from "possibly safe" and from "safe"
- learn specific ways to reduce stress
- affirm eroticism between men, and respect the positive feelings that motivate people to be sexual
- accept that change is not easy or always steady
- recognize that it's human to take risks

The group will meet once a week, co-led by a therapist, Walter Hildner, M.S.W., and a health educator, Michael Gross, Ph.D. For further information, contact **GAY AND LESBIAN COUNSELING SERVICE**, (617) 542-5188.

Weekdays 10 am - 9 pm   *Sliding fee scale/ insurance accepted*   *GLCS is a non-profit corporation*
Confidential services   *No one denied services for inability to pay*   *All insurance claims filed under CSI*

The Guide To Gay New England
January 1987
[Author's Collection]

An Alternative Music Program Seen Weekly On Cable TV

Week of

August 8 **Mission of Burma's** last Boston concert at the Bradford Ballroom.

August 15 **Minor Threat** and **The Stranglers** in concert and a video by **The Fabulous Billygoons.**

August 22 Concert footage of **The Anti-Nowhere League** and **The Proletariat.**

August 27 Coverage of the Finals of the 4th Annual WBCN/Spit Rock and Roll Rumble featuring **Til Tuesday** and **The Sex Execs.**

Sept. 5 An interview with **The Violent Femmes,** concert footage of **D.Y.S.** and a video by **Kraut.**

town	cable channel	day & time
East Boston Charlestown	A52	Thur. 7:00 p.m.
Lexington	A3	Mon. & Thur. 8:00 p.m.
Arlington	3	Tue. & Thur. 9:00 p.m.
Somerville	3	Fri. 8:30 p.m.
Burlington Stoneham Woburn Wilmington Billerica	6	Wed. 5:30 p.m. Sat. 6:00 p.m.

For more information, contact Eric Melcher
Adams-Russell Cablevision, Lexington, MA
(617) 862-7720

Boston Rock magazine
August 1983
[Author's Collection]

Have you heard it?

WCOZ STEREO 94½

Clark, "Capt." Ken Shelton, & Lesley.

BOSTON'S BEST ROCK

Real Paper
October 1, 1975
[David Bieber Archives]

Nebula magazine
December 1971
[David Bieber Archives]

WBCN   Stereo 104

Family Radio

at BRADFORD HOTEL

ROOF DINNER — THEATRE

Now thru Sat. Dec. 30

DAGMAR

Starring in Al Capp's Musical Hit

"LI'L ABNER"

- Complete 2-Hour Musical Comedy
- Dinners from $5.95
- Dancing before and after show

BEFORE THE SHOW TRY:

THE PLACE FOR STEAK

For quick service to enable you to make curtain-time, or for leisure dining in a serene atmosphere.

Featuring the finest steaks and other dishes

Wilbur Theater program

December 18, 1961

[Author's collection]

The Real Paper

May 21, 1981

[David Bieber Archives]

THREE THINGS TO LOOK FOR IN SEAFOOD DINING

◆ FRESHNESS ◆ PREPARATION ◆ PRICE

OR LOOK FOR

T.T. the Bear's Place

"Best Bargain Brunch"
          --The Real Paper

Sundays 10:30 - 4

Cocktail Hour 4 - 7 PM
Happy Hour Prices
Oyster Bar

10 Brookline St. Central Sq. Cambridge
492-0082   Valet Parking

Deep in the heart of Allston lives a super-market – not merely a food store but a food DEMOCRACY, where bulk grains, greens, spices, coffees and teas humbly call out for self-selection and humans with assorted food preferences. Fill mobile food receptacles with everything from organic onions to the lone hamburger patty.

INTRODUCING

The Super Market for the '80's

Get your mobile food

Now all you have to do to shop here is to stop here!

449 CAMBRIDGE ST. ALLSTON
787-1416

Check out a free
3 lb. bag
McIntosh Apples
with any $5 purchase

Kenmore Comet newspaper

November 15, 1984

[Wayne Valdez Archives]

Night Time

November 1974

[David Bieber Archives]

Rathskellar ——— Joe's Kitchen

528 Commonwealth Ave., Kenmore Sq. Boston (617) 536-2750

Fri.-Sat. — "Autumn Blue"
———
Daily Happy Hour 5-7 P.M.
Super Happy Hour 5-7 P.M. Fri.

SEA FOOD
ITALIAN SPECIALTIES
SANDWICHES
SIDE ORDERS
———
DELICIOUS ENTREES

T.V. SPORTS
GAME ROOM

KITCHEN OPEN
11 A.M. - 3 P.M.
Daily Luncheon Specials

UGLY RADIO IS DEAD!

ROCK

WBCN FM   104.1

New England Scene magazine

December 1968

[Kay Bourne Archives at Emerson College:
Iwasaki Library, Special Collections.]

Beautiful moments.

We bring them to you
all day every day.

WSSH
fm 99
Your 'Wish' for Beautiful Music.

Boston Magazine

July 1979 | [David Bieber Archives]

The SWORD IN the STONE COFFEE HOUSE
13 CHARLES ST. BOSTON (COR. BEACON)
"... WHERE the GREATS begin ..!
PRESENTS A
ONE NIGHT ONLY - SPLIT-GIG
SAT. OCT 28 1967 SPECIAL
PAUL McNEIL OPEN 7:30PM
BILL MADISON
MUSIC & SETS AT 8,9,10+11
CHARGE $2.00 PHONE 523-9168

PAUL: MUSIC WITH A MESSAGE, THE MOD-
ERN TOUCH BASIC IN SCOPE; BOSTON'S
OWN BEST KNOWN FOLKSTER.
                   AND
BILL: FAST RISING STAR IN HIS ADOPTED
HOME, BOSTON; SKILL AND FEELING
MARK HIS WRITING AND SINGING...
...WHO WERE RECENTLY 'DISCOVERED'
AT THE 'STONE' AND SIGNED TO LONG
TERM CONTRACTS BY A MAJOR RECORD-
ING STUDIO. WE ARE PROUD TO HAVE
CONTRIBUTED TO THE RECOGNITION OF
THIS TALENTED DUO WHOSE WORKS
SHALL DO MUCH TO REVITALIZE THE
LOCAL BOSTON 'FOLK' SCENE...

COME EARLY: SEATING CAPACITY
LIMITED. SHOWS AT 8:00 and 10:00

Broadside magazine
October 25, 1967
[David Bieber Archives]

"Third Explosive Week!"

WHAT HAPPENS WHEN A BROTHER AND A SISTER BREAK THE ULTIMATE TABOO?

FIREWORKS WOMAN

STARRING
SARAH NICHOLSON

X
COLOR

FOR LADIES AND GENTLEMEN

10,11:20, 12:40 2:00, 3:20, 4:40, 6, 7:20 8:40, 10:00

"97% COMPLETELY UNIQUE PORN!"
Al Goldstein

"SENSUALITY RIGHT OUT OF THE PAGES OF PENTHOUSE AND OUI."
Al Goldstein

"FIREWORKS WOMAN FILLS THE SCREEN WITH A SLEW OF SIZZLING SHOCKERS AND EYEBROW RAISERS." Bob Salmaggie, WINS

"Third Steaming Week!"

HAND IN HAND FILMS
BRINGS YOU THE MEN NO ONE ELSE COULD...
IN THE FILM NO ONE ELSE COULD MAKE!

KEITH ANTHONY MAKES "BIJOU'S" BIG BILL HARRISON LOOK LIKE TOM THUMB!

TIM CHRISTIE MAKES IT IN THE BACK ROW, THE FRONT ROW, OR ANYWHERE ELSE!

CATCHING UP
plus
The Night Before

THEY'RE BOTH
10:10, 11:20, 2:15, 5:10, 8:05, 11:00

Featuring TIM CHRISTIE
COLOR / X RATED / ALL MALE CAST HAND IN HAND FILMS PRODUCTION
Directed by TOM DeSIMONE

free coffee   private lounge

ART CINEMA 1-2
204 Tremont St. 482-4661

garden Cinema   536 9477
19 Arlington St.   OPP. PUBLIC GARDEN

You might forgive him if he were with another woman. Could you go one step further?

SATURDAY NIGHT AT THE BATHS

HERS HIS HIS

[R] RESTRICTED

3RD SMASH WEEK!

SHOWS DAILY AT 2-3:40-5:30-7-8:30-10

NO. STATION ● 1 ● 227-0513

A HAND-IN-HAND FILMS RELEASE
EXCLUSIVE FIRST RUN

THE FIRST ANIMATED GAY FEATURE...

"DEMI GODS"
—PLUS—

The American Adventures of **SURELICK HOLMS**

X

SO. STATION 423-4340

① the damming elements of devil
x
LEVIS' N LEATHER
X

② **"RANCH SLAVES"** —and— **"TARZAN"**
CONTINUOUS SHOWS

THE GAY GUY'S GUIDE

Real Paper
October 1, 1975
[David Bieber Archives]

[November & December 1981]

JACKS
952 Mass Av, Camb.
Tel. 491-7800

Sat – Nov 28
DOWNTIME
with HYPE HORNS

Sun – Nov 29
The Groceries
plus
Suade Cowboys

Mon – Nov 30
Vas deferens
plus
THE DECODERS

Tues – Dec 1
FUNK NITE with
Double Quality

Wed – Dec 2
Natural Boogie

Thu – Dec 3
HYPERTENSION

Fri – Dec 4
Angry Young Bees
plus
LYNN LA PRAD

Sat – Dec 5
Angry Young Bees
plus
Planet Street

Sun – Dec 6
SELLI'S DELI

[February & March 1982]

The World Famous
HONEY LOUNGE
"Bottom of the Hub"

Fri 19
M.I.A.'s
from NYC...
Ozone

Sat 20
Boston Rock presents...
Sex Execs
21-645
Proletariat

Sun 21
Psycho
Annoyed

Wed 24
Boo Boo

Thu 25
007

Fri 26
Future Dads

Sat 27
Limbo Race
Unction

Wed March 3
Little Deers
Disarray

Thu 4
Ice Age

Fri 5
Liquid

Sat 6
Boys Life
Prime Movers

Thu 11
album release party...
amoebas in chaos

Fri 12
Marky Mussel
and the Clams
Real Kids

Sat 13
WLYN...
Dangerous Birds
and guests

909 Boylston St., Boston 536-3136

GREEN STREET STATION

131 Green Street
Jamaica Plain

THU. 10/30	**The Pixies** w/**The Turquoise Bros.**
FRI. 10/31	**The Five, Valdez the Sinner,** and **The Gorehounds**
SAT. 11/1	**Beachmasters, Malarians, Dark Cellars**
SUN. 11/2	2PM-5:30PM **Lecco's Lemma Live All Ages Rap Party, Entertainment TBA $4.00** 7:30PM-10:30PM **Kookaburra Coffeehouse**
THU. 11/6	**Life On Earth** w/ **The Train**
FRI. 11/7	**Titanics** w/ spec. guests
SAT. 11/8	**The Vipers, The Bags & The Time Beings $4.00**
SUN. 11/9	2PM-5:30PM **Lecco's Lemma Live All Ages $4.00** 9PM **Amyl & the Icons**
THU. 11/13	**Allison D.** and spec. guests
FRI. 11/14	**Incredible Casuals, Circle Sky, Ray Mason**
SAT. 11/15	**The Zulus, The Stingers, The Kessels**
SUN. 11/16	2PM-5:30PM **Lecco's Lemma Live All Ages $4.00** 7:30PM-10:30PM **Kookaburra Coffeehouse**
THU. 11/20	**By Design** w/ spec. guests
FRI. 11/21	**Treat Her Right, The Boogey Men** & spec. guests
SAT. 11/22	**The Noise 5th Anniversary Party** w/**The Five, Moving Targets, Slaughter Shack**
SUN. 11/23	**Amyl & the Icons**
FRI. 11/28	**A tribute to Jimi Hendrix on his birthday** featuring **World of Distortion** & spec. guests
SAT. 11/29	**Lecco's Lemma Live. Over 21 Rap Party**
SUN. 11/30	2PM-5:30PM **Lecco's Lemma Live All Ages $4.00** 7:30PM-10:30PM **Kookaburra Coffeehouse**

CONVENIENTLY LOCATED ON THE ARBORWAY LINE AND THE ORANGE LINE, BETWEEN WASHINGTON AND CENTRE ST.'S IN JAMAICA PLAIN. Booking and club info: (617) 436-7209

[October / November 1986]

[May 1981]

RYLES

UPSTAIRS

Thurs., May 14
The Boo Bettes
Fri. & Sat., May 15 & 16
Bellvista
Sun., May 17
Leon Collins
Jazz Tap Revue
Mon., May 18
Klezmer
Conservatory Band
Tues., May 19
Robin Walsh with
Alan Sorvall
Wed., May 20
Slap Happy

DOWNSTAIRS

Thurs., May 14
Robert Merrill Quartet
Fri. & Sat., May 15 & 16
Herman Johnson
Quartet
Sun., May 17
Larry Klug Trio
Mon., May 18
Millie McFaddon
Quartet
Tues. & Wed.,
May 19 & 20
Ed Perkins Trio

CAFE • BAR   876-9330

INMAN SQUARE • CAMBRIDGE

LULU WHITE

3 Appleton St.
Boston • MA
(617) 423-3652

Thursday, Feb. 26
SHANE CHAMPAGNE & THE UPSTARTS

Friday-Sunday,
Feb. 27-March 1
Dance and boogie to the
greatest jazz pianist of all!

DOROTHY DONEGAN TRIO

Monday & Tuesday,
March 2 & 3
MILI BERMEJO
Mexico City's hottest jazz
vocalist. $2.00 cover charge.
featuring
Vinnie Johnson on drums.

Ash Wednesday,
March 4
THE LIARS & THE MIRRORS

Thursday, March 5
NERVOUS EATERS & THE OUTLETS

Valet Parking
Sunday Jazz Brunch
BERT SEAGER TRIO

[February & March 1981]

'PHLUPH'
SOPHISTICATED MADNESS
MGM AND WARNER BROS.
RECORDING & FILM STARS
Complete Psychedelic
Light Shows
THE ECHO
NEW HARD ROCK SCENE
North Beacon St., Brighton

Boston After Dark
April 30, 1969
[Author's Collection]

[February 1986]

CANTAB LOUNGE
738 Massachusetts Ave., Cambridge, MA
354-2685
Under One Roof
— UPSTAIRS —

WEDNESDAY
"Memories..." An evening with
LITTLE JOE COOK TRIO
THURS. Thru SATURDAY
LIVE ENTERTAINMENT
FEATURING
The Peanut Man
LITTLE
JOE
COOK
and The THRILLERS
from 9 p.m. till 2 a.m.

DOWNSTAIRS
DISCO
"THE DANCING D.J."
BERNIE STRICKLAND
EVERY THURS. — FRI. — SAT.
Free admission with this ad

523-9160
Chet's LAST CALL!
— Open 'til 2 am. —

Sat., Sept. 7
THE END
THE NATIONALS
PEELING AUTUMN
BATTERY BRIDGE

Sun., Sept. 8
T.B.A.

Wed., Sept. 11
EASY GOING GUYS

Thurs., Sept. 12
THE HEARD
CORSAIRS • PG-13

Fri., Sept. 13
Late Risers Club Party
with
THE GOSPEL BIRDS
CAPTURE THE FLAG
BLACK CAT BONE

Sat., Sept. 14
PAJAMA SLAVE DANCERS

Sun., Sept. 15
THE GIVENS
NUCLEAR THEATER

Across from the Boston Garden
Over the Penalty Box Lounge
Causeway St., North Station

[September 1985]

WASTED MAN, INC., LYE-SURGE ENTERPRISES
presents
ONLY BOSTON APPEARANCE
LIVE-IN CONCERT

CHARLES LLOYD QUARTETTE
and JAMES COTTON BLUES BAND

BACK BAY THEATER
SAT., NOV. 4, 8:30 P.M. TICKETS $4.50-$3.50-$2.50
THEATRE BOX OFFICE, MAIL ORDER; B.U. STUDENT UNION, I.F.C.; ALL TICKET AGENCIES
E. U. WURLITZER; LIKE NOTHING ELSE; HEADQUARTER EAST AND CLUB 47

Boston After Dark
November 1, 1967
[Author's Collection]

EYEforanEYE AND
POIN T BLANK

AT
THE RAT
528 COMM. AVE   KENMORE SQ.

SATURDAY JANUARY
28th
2:00pm

ALL AGES!!
A TOM + JERRY PRODUCTION

Concert flyer
January 1989
[David Bieber Archives / Chuck White]

Real Paper

October 1, 1975

[David Bieber Archives]

Sweet Potato magazine
May 1984
[Author's Collection]

Celebrity Awards program ad
October 1980
[Kay Bourne Archives at Emerson College:
Iwasaki Library, Special Collections.]

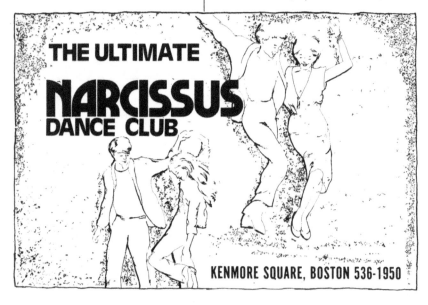

Broadside magazine

February 14, 1968

[David Bieber Archives]

BRIGGS & BRIGGS

established in 1890
For All Your Folkmusic Needs

GIBSON GUITARS

J-45 J-50 LGO

SJ SJN HUMMINGBIRD

MARTIN GUITARS

D-18 D-28

SITARS

COMPLETE LINE

OF ACCESSORIES

RECORDS – LP's & 45's
All traditional & contemporary folk artists
in stock

RECORDERS & RECORDER MUSIC
Kueng, Pelikan, Heinrich, Adler, Her-
wiga, Purcell, Dolmetsch

OPEN 9 – 6, Monday – Saturday

1270 Mass. Ave., Harvard Square, Cambridge
KI 7-2007

"MR. DISCO"
FIRST TIME IN
BOSTON!

"Mr. Disco" turns any
normal event into a
"Disco Dream"
* Singles organizations — pool
parties — apartment parties
— graduations — wedding
receptions — grand openings
— civic events — private
parties.
* Complete sound system and
light show
* We supply everything — you
supply the "people"
* We guarantee our work

Be the host with the
"Smash" party of the
year. Don't wait! Call
Now to find out why we
are #1.

Call "MR. DISCO"

367-8190

Boston Phoenix

July 4, 1978

[David Bieber Archives]

SHEAR CREATIONS HAIR SALON

BOSTON'S FIRST SALON FOR ROCKERS !

tanning

trims

Perms

color

manicures

waxing

supplies

$5.00 off first cut or trim – 10 min from boston !

46 HAMILTON, SAUGUS, MA.   617–233–3823
CURRIER PLAZA

Boston Rock
In fanzine
July 1987
[David Bieber
Archives]

Samson & Delilah
Unisex Salon

860 Beacon Street
Boston
266-7750 or 247-7619
Open 6 days weekly

WE USE AND SELL

Jhirmack

NUCLEIC ACID
BEAUTY PRODUCTS

Boston Magazine
August 1977
[Author's Collection]

Win a fabulous shopping spree for your new face.

1st prize-$100 • 2nd prize-$50 • 3rd prize-$25

Help us celebrate our

GRAND OPENING

Now it's your turn to be beautiful — Register today

MERLE NORMAN
The Place for the Custom Face
144 Newbury Street, Boston (617) 247-4929

Real Paper

June 18, 1981

[David Bieber Archives]

The Two of Clubs ♣♣

823 Main Street Cambridge

Tues. - Sun.
Featuring Top Groups
THE SHEFFIELDS-BOSTON ELECTRIC-THIRD ESTATE
HUMMINGBIRDS-VI SQUAD-INNER•CIRCLE
And
MAGIC

Tues-Ladies Appreciation Night All Drinks .60 8-11
Wed-Senor & Senorita Night All Mexican Drinks .60 a All Night
Thurs-'Hot Pants Night Prizes For 3 Winners All Drinks 8-11 .60

THE IN CELLAR

Mon-Fri Happy Hour 4-7
ALL BAR DRINKS .50

LIVE ENTERTAINMENT
Wednesday-Thursday-Friday

SAT-FREE FOOD
OLDIES BUT GOODIES NIGHT

SUNDAY-SPORTS NIGHT
10 AM-2AM

Your Host
John Courtney

For Information
354-8211

Night Life magazine

October 1973

[David Bieber Archives]

Venus Room

215 CONCORD TURNPIKE ON RT. 2 CAMBRIDGE   AT ASTOR MOTOR INN COMPLEX

Also

Oct. 30 - Nov. 11

" ZAMBOANGA"

6 piece show group

BANNED IN BOSTON   NOV. 13-27

WALTER SCOTT   DEC. 4-18

Tues & Sun - Singles night   **Thurs. Night   Ladies Night**
ALL BAR DRINKS .55°   **ALL LADIES FREE ADMISSION**
Fantastic game room
Your Hosts Andy Crivelli & Chris Scott
Information- 491-1130

Night Life magazine

November 1973

[David Bieber Archives]

Broadside magazine

December 6, 1967

[David Bieber Archives]

Bay State Banner

March 29, 1973

[Kay Bourne Archives at Emerson College: Iwasaki Library, Special Collections.]

Night Life magazine

June / July 1975

[David Bieber Archives]

Golden Banana

617-535-2595

Rt. 1 Peabody, Mass.

This glamourous new nite club features the best national & international show bands

Seating for over 500 –

June 16-22	**WAVE**
June 23-29	**EAST WEST CONNECTION**
June 30-July 6	**TEQUILA SUNRISE "All Girl Band"**
July 7-July 13	**SPICE OF LIFE**
July 14-July 20	**WAYNE COCHRAN**

Las Vegas atmosphere seven nites a week

Concert flyer

October 1989

[David Bieber Archives]

BEN & JERRY'S
ICE CREAM SHOP & SODA FOUNTAIN
840-2 COMMONWEALTH AVE.
KENMORE SQUARE

Kenmore Comet newspaper
November 15, 1984
[Wayne Valdez Archives]

Red Sox game program
1975
[Author's Collection]

STOP! For Fast In And Out Service Before And After The Game!

Around the corner

from the Park

★PizzaPad
★Kenmore
Market
(In The Heart Of Kenmore Sq.)

*PIZZA *SUBS
*KANGAROOS
(Salad Pouch)

Overstuffed
DELI-SANDWICHES
*FRESH FRUITS
*PASTRIES

Convenient Boardwalk Service

FAMOUS DELI SANDWICHES

COZY
ATMOSPHERE

S & S
RESTAURANT

HEARTY,
INEXPENSIVE
HOME-STYLE
MEALS

LARGE SELECTION OF IMPORTED BEER AND WINE

1334 Cambridge Street (Inman Sq.) Cambridge, MA 02139
354-0777   7AM to Midnight all week

The Dolphin Seafood
"the best for the least"

Seafood Platter	$2.95
Steamed Clams	$2.80
Rainbow Trout	$2.85
Swordfish	$3.85

Many other fish delights
Home-made desserts   Fast Take-Out

Open 6 days a week Mon.-Sat. Closed Sunday

1105 Mass. Ave., Cambridge   354-9332

hai hai
JAPANESE RESTAURANT

Bring this invitation to Hai Hai and receive
a $1.00 discount on your next meal

Lunch: noon to 2:30, Mon. through Sat.
Dinner: 5 to 9 PM, seven days a week

423 Boylston St., Boston — 617/536-8474

Green Line to Arlington Station — Exit at Berkeley Street

ふるさとの味

Real Paper
October 1, 1975
[David Bieber Archives]

Kowloon

Venture into the world of the Kowloon restaurant, where fountains whisper and volcanos erupt. Enjoy exotic drinks while you relax under a palm tree or in our mystical Hong Kong Lounge. For dinner, start off with a flaming Pu Pu Platter and end with our sizzling Steak Hawaiian or Special Kowloon Treasure. Dancing to a live band is provided nightly. Luncheon Specials are served seven days a week and Dinner Specials are offered Sunday through Thursday. Try the Kowloon for your next luau, meeting or banquet of up to 475 people.

Route 1, Northbound
Saugus, Mass.
233-0077

Boston Magazine
August 1977
[Author's Collection]

MATTSON ACADEMY OF KARATE

The Mattson Academy invites you   to participate
in a self defense course consisting of five semi-private lessons.

Discover the confidence and feeling of good health

that a Mattson Karate program can give you.

Total price for the course is only $20.00

Call today for further information.   **227-3902**

CONVENIENT LOCATIONS IN:

BOSTON * NEWTON * ARLINGTON * BROCKTON * NORWOOD

Nite Lites magazine
December 1972
[David Bieber Archives]

WE HAVE OVER 100,000 "45" OLDIES IN STOCK.

HERE ARE SOME OF THEM:

COLUMBIA

I PUT A SPELL ON YOU/LITTLE DEMON —
Screamin' Jay Hawkins
GLAD ALL OVER/BITS & PIECES —
Dave Clark Five
SUNSHINE SUPERMAN/MELLOW YELLOW—
Donovan
SUMMERTIME, SUMMERTIME — Jamies
TIME HAS COME TODAY/I CAN'T TURN
YOU LOSE — Chambers Brothers
BATTLE OF NEW ORLEANS/NORTH TO
ALASKA — Johnny Horton
WHITE SPORT COAT/EL PASO —
Marty Robbins
CRY/LITLE WHITE CLOUD THAT CRIED —
Johnny Ray
RUBY BABY/DONNA, THE PRIMA DONNA —
Dion Di Muci
BIG BAD JOHN/LITTLE BLACK BOOK —
Jimmy Dean
DANCE TO THE MUSIC/LIFE —
Sly & the Family Stone
GO AWAY LITTLE GIRL — Steve Laurence
MR. TAMBOURINE MAN/ALL I REALLY
WANT TO DO — Byrds
SOUND OF SILENCE/HOMEWARD BOUND—
Simon & Garfunkel
MERCY MERCY MERCY/DON'T YOU CARE—
Buckinghams

RCA

ARE YOU LONESOME TONIGHT/I GOTTA
KNOW — Elvis Presley
BREAKING UP IS HARD TO DO/NEXT DOOR
TO AN ANGEL — Neil Sedaka
BRING IT ON HOME TO ME/HAVIN' A
PARTY — Sam Cooke
CHAIN GANG/CUPID — Sam Cooke
DON'T BE CRUEL/HOUND DOG—Elvis Presley
END OF THE WORLD/I CAN'T STAY MAD
AT YOU — Skeeter Davis
HEARTBREAK HOTEL/I WAS THE ONE —
Elvis Presley
JAILHOUSE ROCK/TREAT ME NICE —
Elvis Presley
LION SLEEPS TONIGHT/B'WA BABY — Tokens
LOVE IS STRANGE/LOVE IS A TREASURE —
Mickey & Sylvia
OH CAROL/CALENDAR GIRL — Neil Sedaka
GUESS WHO/FUNNY — Jesse Belvin
SHOUT PART I & 2 — Isley Brothers
THREE BELLS/SCARLET RIBBONS—The Browns
YOU SEND ME/TWISTIN' THE NIGHT AWAY
Sam Cooke
CHANGE IS GONNA COME/SAD MOOD —
Sam Cooke
BABY THE RAIN MUST FALL/HONEY WIND
BLOWS — Glenn Yarbrough
RINGO/AN OLD TIN CUP — Lorne Greene

WARNER BROS.
ATLANTIC • ELEKTRA

REMEMBER THEN — Earls
WE BELONG TOGETHER — Robert & Johnny
CHERISH/ALONG COMES MARY —
Association
CATHY'S CLOWN/SO SAD — Everly Brothers
RHYTHM OF THE RAIN/LAST LEAF —
Cascades
SIXTEEN REASONS/MAKE BELIEVE LOVER —
Connie Stevens
PURPLE HAZE/FOXEY LADY — Jimi Hendrix
SHAKE RATTLE & ROLL — Joe Turner
THERE GOES MY BABY — Drifters
HELLO STRANGER — Barbara Lewis
IN THE MIDNIGHT HOUR — Wilson Pickett
WHEN A MAN LOVES A WOMAN —
Percy Sledge
RESPECT — Aretha Franklin
GREEN ONIONS — Booker T. & the M. G.'s
HOLD ON, I'M COMIN' — Sam & Dave
SEARCHIN' — Coasters
YOU KEEP ME HANGING ON —
Vanilla Fudge
GLORIA — Shadows of Knight
TO LOVE SOMEBODY — Bee Gees
SPLISH SPLASH — Bobby Darin
ALLEY CAT — Bent Fabric
MAKE IT WITH YOU — Bread
LOVER'S QUESTION — Clyde McPhatter

OLDIES BUT GOODIES LAND

ASK FOR OUR OLDIES CATALOG!

ASK FOR OUR OLDIES CATALOG!

683 WASHINGTON ST.
(BETWEEN STUART & BOYLSTON STS.)
BOSTON
338—7426
VISIT OUR "SOUL" HEADQUARTERS
SKIPPY WHITE'S RECORDS

1763 WASHINGTON ST. (AT MASS. AVE.),BOSTON ● 2255 WASHINGTON ST.,(AT DUDLEY STATION),ROXBURY;266-1002

Miss Black Fox program ad

June 1975

[Kay Bourne Archives at Emerson College:
Iwasaki Library, Special Collections.]

THE NATIONAL CENTER OF AFRO-AMERICAN ARTISTS

★   PRESENTS AN EVENING OF   ★

SILENT GESTURE - MYSTIC MELODY

Friday and Saturday
JULY 7 - 8, 1978   9:00 P.M.

DYNAMIC PERFORMANCE

FEATURING

FRED JOHNSON
SONG STYLIST AND MIME

IN A DEBUT

CABARET PERFORMANCE

WITH SPECIAL GUEST:

VIVIAN COOLEY

— ● —

MUSIC PERFORMED BY MILT WARD
THE VIRGO SPECTRUM
DISCO DANCING AND REFRESHMENTS
EXOTIC HORS D'OEUVRES

ELMA LEWIS SCHOOL
122 ELM HILL AVE., ROXBURY, MASS.
FOR FURTHER INFORMATION CALL: 442-8820
DONATION $4.00

Event flyer

July 1978

[Kay Bourne Archives at Emerson College:
Iwasaki Library, Special Collections.]

The Avatar

December 8, 1967

[David Bieber Archives]

Allan Day 354-4455
Cheapo Records M&M PRODUCTIONS   PRESENT

ROCK & ROLL

LIVE IN PERSON

sounds good   *arrange for The Harptones*
Paul Cita
212-860-3503

THERE ARE TWO SHOWS
7:30 &10:30 WONDER-
LAND BALLROOM IS
NEXT TO WONDERLAND
STATION ON THE BLUE
LINE AND NEXT TO
WONDERLAND RACETRACK

AMPLE FREE PARKING

FIVE SATINS
IN THE STILL OF THE NIGHT
TO THE AISLE
WONDERFUL GIRL

DUPREES
MY OWN TRUE LOVE
HAVE YOU HEARD
YOU BELONG TO ME

Freddie Paris

FRIDAY
8 DEC
after

HARPTONES
SUNDAY KIND OF LOVE
MEMORIES OF YOU
SINCE I FELL FOR YOU

LIQUOR
SERVED

Willie Winfield lead singer
by Buddy & Ella Johnson

WONDERLAND BLRM REVERE

TICKETS ARE $6 IN ADVANCE $7 AT THE DOOR AND ARE AVAILABLE AT THE FOLLOW-
ING LOCATIONS: WONDERLAND BALLROOM BOXOFFICE TUES,FRI,&SAT 7pm-11pm
CHEAPO RECORDS CAMBRIDGE 354-4455   EVERETT MUSIC EVERETT 389-1220
WALTHAM RECORDS WALTHAM 891-3939   PAN AMERICAN RECORDS ROXBURY 427-9100
MATTAPAN RECORDS MATTAPAN 296-3380   SABLONES RESTAURANT WINTHROP 846-9787
CUSTOM AUTO RADIO SAUGUS 233-3037   INSTANT REPLAY MALDEN 324-9303
PERICOLA'S GIFT SHOP E.BOSTON 567-0115   MUSIC THEATRE WAKEFIELD 246-0704

FOR MORE INFORMATION CALL CHEAPO RECORDS AT 354-4455 OR M&M PRODUCTIONS
AT 329-4825 FOR MAIL ORDER SEND CHECK TO M&M PRODUCTIONS P.O.BOX 716
WESTWOOD MA. 02090 CHECKS PAYABLE TO M&M PRODUCTIONS

Concert Flyer

December 1978

[Kay Bourne Archives at Emerson College:
Iwasaki Library, Special Collections.]

524 RIVER STREET, MATTAPAN SQUARE, MA 02126

Telephone: 298-4417

Weddings - Portraits
Photo Restoration

Commercial Photography & Instant Passport Photos

Elite Designers program ad
Sept 13, 1981
[Kay Bourne Archives at Emerson College:
Iwasaki Library, Special Collections.]

JOHNNY YEE'S
JOHNNY YEE, OWNER

DINNER SPECIAL

HOURS 3 P.M. TO 6 P.M.
SOUP OF THE DAY
BARBECUED CHICKEN WINGS
or EGG ROLL (1)
Choice of One Entree
YUM YUM BEEF
SWEET & SOUR CHICKEN
MIXED VEGETABLES with PORK
SHRIMP with LOBSTER SAUCE
All Above Served with Fried Rice
Tea and Cookies

$3.95

LUNCHEON SPECIAL
A WIDE SELECTION OF
COMBINATION PLATES
From **99¢**

PROUDLY PRESENTS
EVERY SUNDAY & MONDAY
BIG BAND
— JAZZ —
CONCERT
Two Shows Nightly
9 & 11:30

JULY 20-21 STAN KENTON & HIS ORCHESTRA

JULY 27-28 THE PHILIPPINE **KAYUMANGGI**

AUG. 3-4 MAYNARD FERGUSON & HIS ORCHESTRA

AUG. 10-11 THE GLENN MILLER ORCHESTRA

AUG. 17-18 DUKE ELLINGTON ORCHESTRA

AUG. 24-25 DIZZY GILLESPIE

GREAT ENTERTAINMENT EVERY
NIGHT DANCING & FLOOR SHOW
TAMA LEAO and his POLYNESIANS

FOR RESERVATIONS CALL **775-1090**
JOHNNY YEE'S

RESTAURANT & COCKTAIL LOUNGE
228 MAIN ST., W. YARMOUTH
OPEN YEAR ROUND
Dinner Served To 3 A.M.
Fast Take Out Service

CHINESE & AMERICAN FOOD
We Honor All Major Credit Cards

Night Life magazine
July / August 1975
[David Bieber Archives]

LANES OF MATTAPAN

YOUR NEW AFTERWORK PITSTOP!

From 4 pm until 10 pm Monday thru Saturday drink at low, low drink prices.

All beer $1.00
Heineken $1.50
Highballs $1.25
Top Shelf $1.50

Complimentary Hot Entree's!! Delicious Appetite Grabbers

Elegant Food, Inc.

plus
Lanes Features
Gameroom, big screen T.V. and play your daily Lottery number game until 9:45

Ladies Gentlemen Save your	Play Lane's new Happy Hour Game It's easy, It's fun
2 for $1 coupon	
Buy one, get one free Redeem your coupon at Lane's of Mattapan Between 4 pm and 10 pm	Lane's of Mattapan Is open from 4 pm until 2 am

At Lane's it doesn't cost much to have a good time.

Bay State Banner

August 12, 1982

[Kay Bourne Archives at Emerson College: Iwasaki Library, Special Collections.]

Boston Phoenix

September 10, 1985

[David Bieber Archives]

- JAZZ
- BALLET
- MODERN
- TAP
- ETHNIC & MORE
- UNLIMITED CLASSES
- AEROBICS
- NAUTILUS
- FREE WEIGHTS

JAZZ DANCE

BOSTON 542 Commonwealth Ave. 266-6026
CAMBRIDGE 536 Massachusetts Ave. 492-4680
WATERTOWN 23 Main St. 926-2700
WELLESLEY 34 Washington St. 237-6465 (across from Grossman's at Wellesley Racquet Club)
MEDFORD 682 Fellsway 391-2751 (at the Fellsway Shopping Plaza)
NEW YORK 400 Lafayette St. (212)260-7301

Programs and facilities vary with location.

call today! **joy of Movement** ™
DANCE & FITNESS CENTERS
WE GUARANTEE THE BEST VALUE IN TOWN!

HAVE YOU HEARD ?

NATIVE TONGUE	album
MISSION OF BURMA	copyright tape
THE PROLETARIAT	cassette, album
S.S. DECONTROL	edit/sequence e.p. (2)
PRIMARY COLORS	pre-production
POST MODERNS	radio tape
THE FREEZE	e.p.
DREDD FOOLE & THE DIN	single
CLASSIC RUINS	radio tape
THE F.U.'S	mix, e.p.

WE HAVE.

radiobeat

KENMORE SQ., BOSTON
(617) 353-1608 / $15.00 per hour

*Boston Rock
magazine*

July 1983

[Author's
Collection]

1106 BOYLSTON ST., BOSTON
247-2238

We Buy, Sell and Trade New, Used & Rare
LPs & 45s — and now, VIDEO RENTAL, TOO!

The Noise

May 1986

[Author's
Collection]

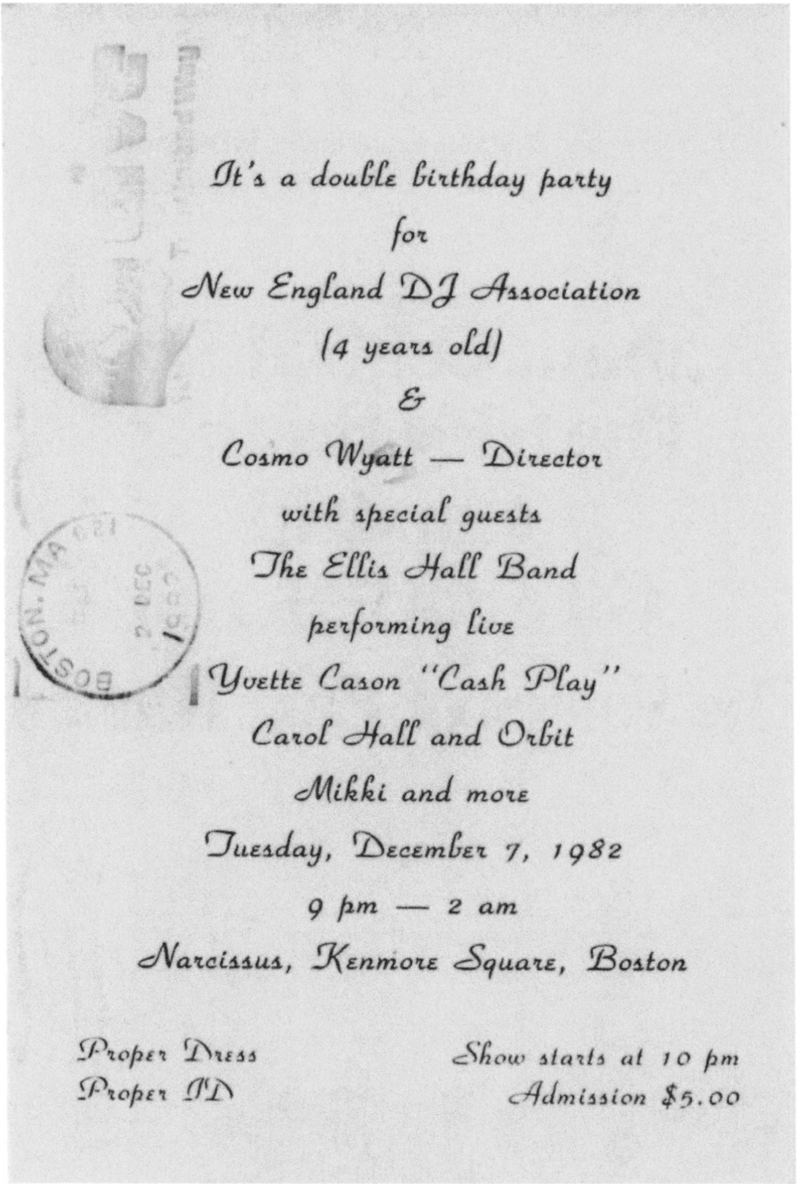

It's a double birthday party

for

New England DJ Association

(4 years old)

&

Cosmo Wyatt — Director

with special guests

The Ellis Hall Band

performing live

Yvette Cason "Cash Play"

Carol Hall and Orbit

Mikki and more

Tuesday, December 7, 1982

9 pm — 2 am

Narcissus, Kenmore Square, Boston

Proper Dress   Show starts at 10 pm
Proper ID   Admission $5.00

Event invite

December 1982

[Kay Bourne Archives at Emerson College:
Iwasaki Library, Special Collections.]

UPTOWN IN THE PARK

Phase II

White Stadium, Franklin Park, Boston
Sunday, August 25 at 2 o'clock in the afternoon

Graham Central Station
The Isley Brothers
Mandrill
Gil Scott-Heron
The Voices of East Harlem

Coming off our first successful festival (see enclosure) in July,
UPTOWN IN THE PARK moves into Phase II in a series of open air
concerts at White Stadium, Franklin Park, Boston. The series is
being produced for the Elma Lewis School of Fine Arts, a division
of the National Center of Afro-American Artists.

Masterworks, 10 Emerson Place, Suite 14e, Boston, Massachusetts 02114   617-262-6666

Concert flyer

August 1974

[Kay Bourne Archives at Emerson College: Iwasaki
Library, Special Collections.]

Boston
After Dark

November 1,
1967

[Author's
Collection]

Real Paper

March 5, 1981

[David Bieber Archives]

Want A Horse?

come to

SUFFOLK DOWNS

You're sure to find some horse that you fancy. Maybe a grey one, or bay one, or perhaps an all black one. You can spend all afternoon getting off on the infinite and subtle color variations of these magnificent creatures. You may even catch horse fever yourself.

Suffolk Downs is more than a Race Track It's a Great Experience.

You owe it to yourself to try it at least once. Pick any Afternoon except Tuesday. We're just a mile past Logan Airport 1st race 1:45 P.M.

Boston After Dark

May 2, 1972

[David Bieber Archives]

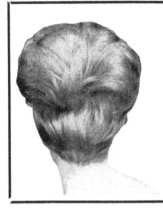

J oyce Christopher

73 NEWBURY ST.

CO 6-6336

The ultimate
look achieved
with a Rayette permanent

PHILADELPHIA - NEW YORK - PARIS

Wilbur Theater program

December 18, 1961

[Author's Collection]

Boston Phoenix

November 15, 1977

[David Bieber Archives]

BERKLEY
DISCO
& STAN'S KITCHEN
173 Mass. Ave., Boston
NOW
INTRODUCING
JUKE BOX
DISCO MUSIC
EAT, DRINK, &
BE MERRY!

The **Robie**
SECRETARIAL
SCHOOL

*1 year's secretarial
training program!*

Expert training in Typing, Shorthand,
English, Accounting, Economics and Office Procedure. Also receive expert finish-
ing guidance in the Social Graces, Ward-
robe, Makeup and Voice, Hairstyling, Fig-
ure Control, Visual Poise and Personality
Development . . . attributes which make
Robie secretaries more valuable and attractive. Placement service and residence
of course.

Call or write to school for brochure.

304 Boylston St., Boston, Mass.
Opposite Public Garden
PHONE CO 7-5080

Boston Advertiser newspaper

Nov 24, 1963

[Author's Collection]

PEOPLE
WHEREVER
THEY MAY BE
EVEN UP A TREE
KEEP IN TOUCH
WITH
'NAC

WNAC RADIO 680

Colonial Theater program ad
August 1961
[Author's Collection]

REGGAE DANCE PARTY

HOUSE OF ASSEMBLY

REGGAE DISCO BY WUNR'S

WHITE RAM

Fri., May 20 & Sat., May 21

THE CLUB

823 MAIN STREET, CENTRAL SQ., CAMB.

TICKETS $2.50 IN ADVANCE AVAILABLE AT
RUPERT'S MUSIC
2BROOKLINE ST., CENTRAL SQ.
$3.00 AT THE DOOR

*The Sporting Life
newspaper*
May 19, 1977

[Kay Bourne Archives
at Emerson College:
Iwasaki Library, Special
Collections.]

*Yvonne Rose
presents Fantasia
82 program ad*
May 16, 1982

[Kay Bourne Archives
at Emerson College:
Iwasaki Library, Special
Collections.]

442-0444

No
MONKEY
BUSINESS
WE GIVE
SERVICE

CORNBREAD'S AQUARIUM

Your family center for fish & pet supplies
MON. THRU THURS. 9 A.M. - 8 P.M.
FRI. & SAT. 9 A.M. - 9 P.M.
SUN. 12 NOON - 6 P.M.
2206 WASH ST. NEXT TO BLAIRS, BOSTON, MA 02119

Event flyer

August 1971

[Kay Bourne Archives at Emerson College:
Iwasaki Library, Special Collections.]

BOSTON AFRO–AMERICAN ARTISTS
PRESENTS
THE 11TH ANNUAL *SATURDAY*
&
SUNDAY   IN THE PARK

JULY 23 & 24TH (11–7 P.M.
MUNROE PARK
Rain date July 30,31

boston afro american artist
presents
an exhibition of paintings,
sculptures, photografhy

ALL ARTIST WELCOME TO ENTER
PRIZES AWARDED BY JURY
FOR INFORMATION CALL 427–0448

on the corners of Townsend, Harold, Munroe & Walnut St.

Event program

July 1977

[Kay Bourne Archives at Emerson College:
Iwasaki Library, Special Collections.]

Boston Rock
magazine

September 1980

[Author's
Collection]

Concert flyer

February 1982

[Courtesy of Gallery East
Productions]

WBCN 104.1 FM
171 Newbury St. Boston
AMERICAN
REVOLUTION

N.E.SCENE
899 Boylston St.

1510 AM **WMEX**
111 Broadway Boston
BROADCAST
HOUSE

HELP US FORM A ROCK'N ROLL* GOVT.

WE ALL JOIN HANDS IN ASKING: WHO DO YOU WANT LEADING YOU?

THIS IS YOUR BALLOT   CHECK YOUR CHOICES
For 1968's only open and honest election.

President	Jimi Hendrix
	Frank Zappa
	John Lennon
	Mick Jagger

Sec. of Defense	Albert King
	John Sebastian
	John Mayall
	Jeff Beck

Vice President	Al Kooper
	Paul McCartney
	Steve Winwood
	Bob Dylan

Speaker of the House	Tiny Tim
	Pig Pen
	Janis Joplin
	Brian Wilson

Sec. of State	Steve Miller
	Eric Clapton
	Gracie Slick
	Marty Balin

Ambassador to	Don Rickles to Red China
Country of your Choice	Tiny Tim to U.S.S.R.
	John Lennon to Japan
	Van Dyke Parks to India

LET US REASON TOGETHER LBJ

*Anyone with rythm!
free ballots at either radio station , the magazine, or their advertisers

New England Scene magazine

December 1968

[Kay Bourne Archives at Emerson College: Iwasaki Library, Special Collections.]

New England Scene magazine
September 1968
[David Bieber Archives]

WHERE PEOPLE WHO LIVE
EXTREMELY WELL AT HOME CAN LIVE EXTREMELY WELL
AWAY FROM HOME.

THE RITZ.

THE RITZ-CARLTON, BOSTON   PREFERRED HOTEL RESERVATIONS. 800-323-7500

Boston Magazine
July 1979
[David Bieber Archives]

THE NEGRO REPERTORY THEATRE OF BOSTON
— Presents —

A Reading Performance of a New American Play

"WEIGHED IN THE BALANCE"
by WARREN COLEMAN

FRIDAY EVENING, SEPTEMBER 29, 1967

NEW ENGLAND LIFE HALL
225 Clarendon Street, Boston, Mass.

Staged by Ralf Coleman

▼▼▼

——: P R O G R A M :——

READERS

SENIOR JUDGE ANDERSON _____ PERCY E. JOHNSON, SR.
JUDGE MARSHALL _____ HAROLD BLAIR
JUDGE SILVERSTEIN _____ CHARLES YOUNGER

ATTORNEYS

FOR THE PROSECUTION _____ OSCAR FARMER
FOR THE DEFENSE _____ CHARLES NESBIT

STELLA _____ ADENA LAKE
CARLA _____ CLAUDIA DENBY
MRS. EVERETT _____ ADA ROSTON
MRS. SCHUENBERG _____ VIRGINIA SHELDON

JOE _____ MARVIN WATSON
BARRETT _____ LIONEL LINDSAY, JR.

NARRATION BY THE AUTHOR.   All readers, except the Judges, and Attorneys for the Prosecution and Defense will read other parts.

———

THE AUTHOR, Warren Coleman, studied voice in Boston, and started his career here as a concert baritone.   He played his first starring role on Broadway in 1934, as "John Henry", in the musical drama, "Roll Sweet Chariot."   At auditions in Boston, he was next chosen by George Gershwin to play the lead role of "Crown," in the original company of "Porgy & Bess".   With acclaim from press and public he sang this dramatic role on Broadway and on tour for many years.   His next success was a singing lead in "Lost in the Stars", with Todd Duncan.   Followed a memorable portrayal of "Frank", in the long-run comedy hit "Anna Lucasta".   He has had his own little theatre in Harlem; wrote, produced and directed a full length movie, "Carib Gold," with Ethel Waters.   He has written many full length plays.   An early one, "The Greener Grass" was produced in Boston some years ago.   Among others are: "Salt & Pepper To Taste", Sleeping Sickness", and "Darling, Don't Integrate My Husband."   He now resides on Martha's Vineyard and devotes most of his spare time to writing for the stage, movies and television.

———

Ushers: Gretchen Wortham and Marcia Joyner

Next N. R. T. Production —"Tambourines To Glory"- by Langston Hughes

Theater program page

September 1967

[Kay Bourne Archives at Emerson College: Iwasaki Library, Special Collections.]

Roxbury Community College course flyer

Spring 1983

[Kay Bourne Archives at Emerson College: Iwasaki Library,
Special Collections.]

Boston Advertiser newspaper

November 24, 1963

[Author's Collection]

Event flyer

October 1984

[Wayne Valdez Archives]

P. O. Box 612   Roxbury, Mass. 02119

**NEW ENGLAND AFRICAN - AMERICAN ART
AND MUSIC ASSN. AND COFFY PRODUCTIONS**

— PRESENT —

A REGGAE - FUNK DISCO

**TO BENEFIT
COOPER CTR. ATHLETIC DEPT.**

FRIDAY, MARCH 13, 1981

10:00 P.M. - 4:00 A.M.

PLACE:

THE DENNISON HOUSE
3RD FLOOR
**584 COLUMBIA ROAD
COR. COLUMBIA RD. AND DUDLEY ST.
DORCHESTER, MASS.**

MUSIC BY

HAROLD AUSTIN - WRBB
GLENDALE REID - WRBB

Minimum Age 20   . . .
I.D. Required   **(CASH BAR)**
TICKETS $3.00 ADV.   **$4.00 AT DOOR**

TICKET INFORMATION:
445-1813 MR. HART, MR. WILLIAMS, MR. HEARNS
427-3953 · COFFY PROD.

Bay State Banner

March 12, 1981

[Kay Bourne Archives at Emerson College: Iwasaki Library,
Special Collections.]

You Are Cordially Invited To Attend The

9th Anniversary Celebration

of

LANE'S of Mattapan

1354 Blue Hill Avenue

Sunday, July 19, 1981 — Starts at 7:00 P.M,

— *Special Guest* —

— *Featuring Live and In Person* —

THE ENERGETICS

James A. Lewis III, M.C.

Champagne - Hors D'Oeurves   1st Show 7:30 pm

Event invite

July 1981

[Kay Bourne Archives at Emerson College:
Iwasaki Library, Special Collections.]

Boston Jazz
The Way We Are.

JAZZ ON THE RADIO

Daily shows:	M-F	7am-11:30am	WBUR	"New Morning" w/Charlie Perkins
	M-F	8am-10am	WHRB	"Breakfast Jam"
	M-F	5:30pm-7pm	WHRB	"Jazz Entree"
	M-F	2am-6am	WBCN	"Eric Jackson Show"
MONDAY		5pm-8pm	WRBB	
		7pm-8pm	WHRB	"The Gospel Hour"
		9:30-midnite	WTBS	"Jazz n Such"
		10pm-1am	WBUR	"Ed Beach"/ "Just Jazz"
		midnite-1am	WGBH	"The Real New Orleans"
TUESDAY		7pm-8pm	WHRB	"Ebony Patterns"
		9:30-midnite	WTBS	
		10pm-1am	WBUR	"Just Jazz"/ Ed Beach
		11:15pm-1am	WBCN	"Live from Jazz Workshop"
		11:15pm-1am	WGBH	"Jazz Round Midnite"
		midnite	WMFO	
WEDNESDAY		2pm-5pm	WERS	
		7pm-8pm	WHRB	"Juke" (blues)
		midnite	WGBH	"What's New in Jazz"
THURSDAY		7pm-8pm	WHRB	"Backtracking"
		10pm-midnite	WMFO	
		10pm-1am	WBUR	"Jazz Cove"
		11:15pm-1am	WGBH	"Jazz Round Midnite"
FRIDAY		7pm-8pm	WHRB	"Rhythm n Blues"
		8pm-9pm	WGBH	"The Real New Orleans
		9pm-10:30pm	WGBH	"The Jazz Decades"
		10pm-1am	WBUR	"Jazz Corner"
		10:30pm-midnite	WGBH	"Jazz Performance"
SATURDAY:		2-5pm	WBUR	"The Awakening" w/Wylie Rollins
		4-7pm	WTBS	"Jazz Celebration" w/Justin Freed & Rich Seidel
		8pm-midnight	WHRB	"Sound of Jazz"
		11pm-1am	WBUR	"Jazz in the Night"
		midnite	WHRB	"Jazz Round Midnite"
		1am-8am	WCRB	"The Grotto" w/Oscar Jackson
SUNDAY		2-4pm	WTBS	"Jazz Traditional" w/ Dave Luckman
		4-5pm	WTBS	"Gospel Train" w/Skippy White
		7-9pm	WTBS	"Inward Voyage"
		9pm-2am	WBUR	"Spaces" w/Steve Elman
		midnite	WTBS	"The Ghetto"
		11pm-12:30am	WGBH	"The Jazz Decades"

JAZZ IN THE CLUBS AROUND TOWN [call for specifics]

Jazz Workshop	733 Boylston St., Boston	nightly	267-1300
Wally's	428 Mass. Ave, Boston	wkends	267-9551
Zircon	298 Beacon, Somerville	Tues's	354-9242
Debbie's	Merrimac St., Boston		
Orson Welles	1001 Mass Ave., Cambridge		868-3607
Scotch Sirloin	Washington St., Boston		723-3677
Estelle's	888 Tremont St., Roxbury		427-0200

When in New York City Call "JAZZLINE" (211)421-3592
for all information.

Driving Wheel magazine

March 1, 1974

[David Bieber Archives]

The Institute of Contemporary
Art and The Boston Phoenix
present

Jean Cocteau
Film Retrospective
Through August 25

Thursday, July 6 - Friday, July 7
THE ETERNAL RETURN (1943)

Directed by Jean Delannoy.
Written by Jean Cocteau. With Jean Marais, Madeline
Sologne.
Cocteau begins his tradition of modern dress versions of
timeless mythology with this transposition of the classic
Breton legend of Tristan and Iseult.
100 minutes. Complete shows 7 pm & 9 pm, & Friday
Noon.

Thursday, July 13 - Friday, July 14
ORPHEUS (1949)

Written and directed by Jean Cocteau.
With Jean Marais, Francois Perrier, Maria Casares.
"The masterpiece of magical filmmaking. Though a
narrative treatment of the legend of Orpheus is a modern
Parisian setting, it is as inventive and enigmatic as a dream
. . . The motorcyclists are part of a new mythology, they
suggest images of our time: secret police . . . black heroes
. . . agents of some unknown authority . . . executioners
. . . visitors from outer space . . . the irrational . . . This
gives the violence and mystery of the Orpheus story a
kind of contemporaneity that, in other hands, might seem
merely chic; but Cocteau's special gift was to raise chic to
art." — Pauline Kael.
86 minutes. Complete shows 7 pm & 9 pm, & Friday
Noon.

Cocteau T-Shirts

A limited edition of T-shirts celebrating the Jean
Cocteau film retrospective are available at the
screenings and at the ICA shop during the week
(exc. Mon.) between 10 and 5 pm.

ICA 955 Boylston Street Boston 02115 (617) 266-5151
Admission to films $2.00/$1.50 for ICA members

Boston Phoenix
July 4, 1978
[David Bieber Archive]

M'LADY'S LIB CAFE

The Sporting Life newspaper

May 19, 1977

[Kay Bourne Archives at Emerson College: Iwasaki Library, Special Collections.]

WHERE THE HAPPY PEOPLE MEET

Kitchen open nightly...

1162 Blue Hill Ave. Parking in the rear

EVERY NIGHT IS LADIES NIGHT AT THE LIB

FOR THE BEST IN HOME COOKING DINE WITH
JOHNNIE MAE WHITE

Home Made Cakes & Pies And, all sorts of goodies

Kitchen Open:
Tues. & Wed. — 12 noon - 9 p.m.
Thurs. & Fri. — 12 noon - midnight
Saturday — 12 noon - 11 p.m.

November Benefits for the AIDS Action Committee

Thursday, Nov. 19
**OPENING NIGHT OF CLUB CABARET
AT CLUB CAFE**
featuring
THE TEN PERCENT REVUE
Tickets available at Club Cafe
For more information call **(617) 536-0966**

Friday, Nov. 20
KISS-108 FM & WBZ-TV Channel 4
present
JAY LENO Live
at Symphony Hall
10:30 pm
Tickets $30, $28, $26

Sunday, Nov. 22
LET'S TWIST AGAIN
Featuring CHUBBY CHECKER Live
at the NYC Jukebox in Boston
275 Tremont Street
8 pm
Tickets $25 in advance, $30 at the door
Available at Club Cafe, Jukebox, Bostix, & Copley Flair

Special **JUNE CLEAVER**
**DINNER
at CLUB CAFE**
with Hot Rod Limo Service
to the Party and Show
$75 Dinner
Available only at Club Cafe

The Guide To The Gay Northeast
November 1987
[Author's collection]

RECORDS

presents

JAYHAWK!
The New 12" Single From
Sir Jake

ON SALE AT: Skippy White's, Mattapan Records, Tower Records, Cheapo's, Nubian Notions, The Coop, City Cassette, Looney Tunes, In Your Ear, Newbury Comix, Dance Musik Plus, Rainbow Records in Providence.

For the Freshest in Funky Hip-Hop!

——————WorldWide Management——————
P.O. Box 2104, Jamaica Plain, MA 02130   (617) 522-0791

Boston Rock magazine

April 1988

[Author's Collection]

Boston Rock magazine

February 1982

[Author's Collection]

Suede Cowboys equipment stolen: Fender Rhodes Electric Piano, Serial #S2430; ARP 2600 Synthesizer, Serial #26891; Yamaha Cs5 Synthesizer; Gibson SJN acoustic guitar, D-armand pick-up; Ampeg V4 amp head. Leave message at 424-1233.

GG ALLIN MAKES ME BARFFFF

Leper equipment stolen: Peavy bass amp & cab, Marshall cab & lead amp & Infamous Leper drum set. Any info, please call Kev, 437-0058. Thanks.

DON'T MISS AN ISSUE! To have High School Times mailed to your house every month, send $3 to HST, 9 Nampus Ave. #8, Acton 01720.

Fashion—Your creations or mine. I will sew for you, your shop or boutique. Enjoy creative, unique work. Alterations too. Eleanor, 524-2742.

ROCK VIDEO Call Red Shark 298-9806 or 749-7732.

Wanted: someone to go out and party. See bands, gab with people and generally have fun because I can't find the time. Don't call us—we'll call you.

Free Records, Books, 3 movies. **Free** vacation in Hollywood. 1982 "Cocaine Sweepstakes ticket." **RUSH $3** to Rose, Box 4934, 367 Newbury St., Boston 02115.

The First Night Of Summer Will Be VERY HOT!

ELLIS HALL GROUP
Wednesday, June 21

967 Comm. Ave., Boston, 254-2052

The Paradise

Real Paper
June 24, 1978
[David Bieber Archives]

The Noise

December 1985

[Author's Collection]

Concert flyer
January 1979
[David Bieber Archives]

food glorious food

Restaurant owners wishing to advertise in this column should contact Miss Horn Boston After Dark (536-5390) concerning rates.

BELGIAN

RUGBYMAN RESTAURANT
Belgian & French Cuisine. All wine imported and your favorite cocktails. Located at the elegant Jamaicaway Towers, 111 Perkins St., Jamaica Plain. Hours 5 pm. to 1 am. (except Sun.) Res. 522-0722

SIDEWALK CAFE

CAFE FLORIAN
Boston's authentic continental Sidewalk Cafe, serving European luncheons, pastries and beverages from noon 'til midnight daily, Fri. & Sat. 'til 1 a.m. 85 Newbury Street.

Closed on Sun.

MEXICAN

CASA MEXICO
75 Winthrop St., Camb. Open Sun-Thurs. 6 to 10 p.m. Fri. & Sat. 6 to 11 p.m. Call 491-4552 for reservations.

EL DIABLO
7a Mt. Auburn Street, Cambridge. Informal atmosphere, reasonable prices. Dinner: tacos, enchiladas, brown rice, y otras cosas. Open 7 days a week 5-10 p.m.

HUNGARIAN

CHARDAS
Authentic Hungarian Cuisine Wines & cocktails. 1306 Beacon, Brookline, Coolidge Corner. Reservations 232-3596. Dinner from 5:30, Sundays from 4:30.

EAST-WEST

SANAE
Unique combination: oriental and pioneer American styles. Grain dinners, fresh vegetables, seafood, desserts. 272 Newbury St., Bos. Tues-Sun 3-10. Fri-Sat 3-11. 247-8434.

STEAK

"GEORGE 'N NICK'S"
Prime steaks charcoal-broiled as you wait: shish-ka-bob. Beer & Wine. Student luncheons. Open 11:00 am-10 pm, Mon-Sat. Res: 354-9700. In Central Sq., 569 Mass Ave., Camb.

INDIAN

INDIA SWEET HOUSE
243 Hampshire St., Camb. (Inman Sq.) 354-0949
Authentic, excellent currys, home-made breads, exotic appetizers, delicious desserts, full-course dinners as low as $1.70 Open 6 to 9 p.m. Fri. and Sat. 'til 10 p.m.

GREEK

ATHENIAN TAVERNA
"A touch of Athens comes to Central Square." Modern Greek cuisine and wines; cocktails. Open daily for Lunch and Dinner, 11:30-11:30. Res.: 547-6300. 569 Mass. Ave., Cambridge.

GREEK/AMERICAN

UNIVERSITY RESTAURANT
Featuring Shiskabob cooked over open hearth. Greek salad a specialty. Toga lounge–imported beers and wines. 11 to 10 p.m. Daily except Sunday, 1276 Mass. Ave., Harvard Sq.

JAPANESE

TEMPURA HUT
The Finest in Japanese Cuisine. Tempura Sukiyaki, Yaki-Tori Shahimi. 7 Mt. Auburn St., Cambridge. 12 to 10 p.m. Daily & Sun. UN 8-0551

SEAFOOD

HALF-SHELL
743 Boylston St., across from the Pru. Finest seafoods and cocktails. Open 'til 2 a.m. Food served 'til closing. 423-5555.

LEGAL SEAFOODS
Seafood fresh from our own fish market. Wonderfully informal atmosphere and the best seafood you've ever tasted. Luncheon special - Fish and Chips Dinner 99c. Open Tues. through Sat., 11 a.m. - 9 p.m., 237 Hampshire St., Inman Sq., Cambridge 354-8473.

SEA SHELL RESTAURANT
146 Tremont Street, across from the Common. Specializing in seafood with fine liquors. Open for luncheon at 11:00 a.m. Dinner served til closing at 1:00 a.m. 482-5483

ITALIAN

VILLA CAPRI
At Inman Square, Cambridge Florentine Cuisine. Open daily for Luncheons & Dinner 11:30-11:30. For Res., call TR 6-9330.

Boston After Dark

Oct 1, 1969

[David Bieber Archives]

HENRY SYPHER'S
AQUATIC AQUARIUM
PET & PLANT SHOP

We carry EVERYTHING you need to start,
stock and maintain your fresh or salt
water aquarium

Live plants and birds add to the unique
environment of our shop. We welcome you
to come in and look around.

Ask about group and organization discounts

The classiest and most complete tropical
and marine fish, pet and plant
supply house in the area.

Custom Aquariums

566 COLUMBIA ROAD, at Uphams Corner
DORCHESTER, MASS. 02125
436-2666

Henry Sypher, *Proprietor*
Daily thru Saturday 11 AM to 7 PM

Massachusetts Association of Afro-American Police banquet program ad
October 1982
[Kay Bourne Archives at Emerson College: Iwasaki Library, Special Collections.]

K SIRRAH

PRODUCTIONS

Lionel Kelley / Eddie Harris (617) 536-9707

Photography by Darryl

BOSTON, MA

Designers Display Competition program ad
March 11, 1983
[Kay Bourne Archives at Emerson College: Iwasaki Library, Special Collections.]

Get Your Nuts Off.

etric Motors

A concern for you and your car.

320 Watertown St., Rear Newton
Tues.-Sat. 244-7826

Specializing in Mercedes and BMW.

Real Paper

April 19, 1980

[David Bieber Archives]

Boston University News

October 18, 1973

[David Bieber Archives]

Take a LOOK
at Life.

Prescriptions Filled • Fashion Sunwear •
Large Selection of Frames • Swim Goggles •
Ski Goggles • Diving Masks • Contact Lenses
• Artificial Eyes • Hearing Aids • Soldering on
Metal Frames • Frames Repaired

Our hours: Monday through
Friday, 9 to 5. Saturday, 9
to 1. September to June.
"Free Parking". Our
telephone: LI2-8181.

See us.
MONTGOMERY-FROST-LLOYD'S

*BOSTON'S
EYE STYLE
CENTER*

Boston: 662 Beacon St. • 414 Boylston St. • 3 0 0 Washington St. • Cambridge: Harvard Sq.
Hyannis: Lewis Bay Road • Quincy: 1073 Hancock St. • Norwood: 677-A Washington St.

GIRLS

MAPS

MISSION of BURMA

SAT. SEPT. 29

38 thayer st.

au go-go!

Concert flyer

September 1979

[Courtesy of Peter Prescott]

Concert flyer

April 1985

[David Bieber Archives / Chuck White]

DREZNIAK

and at JONATHAN SWIFTS   APRIL 29th.

Event flyer

June 1989

[Kay Bourne Archives at Emerson College:
Iwasaki Library, Special Collections.]

Fly Down to the Coop & Save on the Entire Flying Dutchman Catalog!

GIL SCOTT-HERON
FREE WILL

GATO BARBIERI-EL PAMPERO
Composer of the Original Music for
"Last Tango in Paris"

ENTIRE
FLYING DUTCHMAN
CATALOG

GATO BARBIERI
UNDER FIRE

LARRY CORYELL
BAREFOOT BOY

$3.57

the Coop

HARVARD SQUARE
M.I.T STUDENT CENTER
CHILDREN'S HOSPITAL MEDICAL CENTER

LEON THOMAS
BLUES & THE SOULFUL TRUTH

OLIVER NELSON
SWISS SUITE

Boston Phoenix
April 24, 1973
[David Bieber Archives]

★ ROSCOE'S ★

"The Total Entertainment Complex"
38 WARREN STREET — ROXBURY, MASS.

coming MAY 15-16-17
ZZ - HILL
Fri., Sat., Sun.

LAURA LEE -
Love Rights Rip Off
APRIL 24-25-26

TED TAYLOR -
Steal Away
May 1-2-3

Every Thurs. at ROSCOE'S
Musicians JAM NIGHT & Do Your Thing Affair

Every Wednesday
The Biggest Ladies Night in New England

For Reservations: Call 427-4115

Catered evening of Hor d'oeuvres & Champagne.
THIS IS A "LOVEMAN PRODUCTION"

Bay State Banner

April 1981

[Kay Bourne Archives at Emerson College:
Iwasaki Library, Special Collections.]

The Sound You've Been
waiting for
RADIO STATION ~ WCAS
Invites You To a Talent
SHOWCASE
at
ROSCOE'S -38 Warren St. ~ Roxbury
Every Thursday ~ 8:30 to 2:00 A.M!
Come Meet the DJ's of WCAS
$CASH Prizes & CHAMPAYNE

FEATURING
LARRY & WOO
HARTBEAT BAND
with your host ~ D.K. GILMORE
Free invitation ~ admits two until
11:00 P.M

Event flyer

Early 1980s

[Kay Bourne Archives at Emerson College:
Iwasaki Library, Special Collections.]

nuArts

PRESENTS

David Murray
Big Band Concert

**Saturday
October 25
8:30 P.M.**

*World premiere produced
by the Jazz Coalition of
Boston in association with
WGBH Radio Boston*

Alumni Auditorium
Northeastern University
360 Huntington Avenue
Boston. Free Parking.

Tickets
$16.50, $14.00
$12.50, $10.00 (Stu/Srs)
Call nuArts Tickets
437-2247
Charg-tix 542-8511
Out of Town Ticket
Agency 492-1900

**A Jazz Legacy Project tribute to tenor sax
greats Paul Gonsalves, Ben Webster, and
Lester Young. Major funding provided by
the Massachusetts Council on the Arts
and Humanities New Works Program. A pres-
entation of the Northeastern University
Division of Fine Arts.**

Boston Phoenix

October 28, 1986

[David Bieber Archives]

[August 1983]

Storyville

Sat Aug. 6
Welcome Back
The Bush Tetras
Fine China

Thurs 11
Funk Night
Hypertension

Fri 12
**Prince Charles and the
City Beat Band**

Rods & Cones

Aug 14-22
Closed For Renovation!

Tues 23
Reopening!
**The Neats
Busted Statues**

Thur 25
**007
Skin**

Fri 26
Jeff & Jane Hudson
with special guests

Sat 27
**Primary Colors
MIA's**

645 BEACON ST.
KENMORE SQ.
ADVENTURES IN ROCK

Bunratty's
186 HARVARD AVE., ALLSTON
254-9804

Sat., Sept. 7	Mon., Sept. 9	Fri., Sept. 13
GARY SHANE AND THE DETOUR plus **BODY POLITICS**	**THE HANDSOME DEVILS** featuring **LARRY BAIDER** and **BILLY KOVER**	**JAMES MONTGOMERY BAND** plus **P.C.B.**

Sun., Sept. 8	Tues., Sept. 10	Sat., Sept. 14
THE WRECKING CREW plus **BLIND LEMON PLEDGE** and **THE SEEING EYE DOGS**	**HEARTS ON FIRE PLEASURE POINT** Wed., Sept. 11 **BALL & PIVOT** plus **THE FABLES** Thurs., Sept. 12 **VISITOR** plus **WIDE ANGLE**	**EXTREME** plus **THE JACKALS** plus **MUGGS** Coming: Sept. 17 **WILLIE "LOCO" ALEXANDER**

Boston's Best Live Rock & Roll — Seven Nights A Week 'Til 2 AM

[September 1985]

Bunratty's
186 Harvard Ave., Allston
254-9820

Sept.

9 & 10 Different Strokes
11-15 Edge City
16 & 17 Billy Colwell
18-22 Home Cookin
23 & 24 Good Foot
25-29 John Lincoln Wright
    & Sour Mash Boys
30   White Mt. Blend

Oct.

1-6 Flyer
7 & 8 Nike Aukuma
9-13 Mitch Chakour
14 & 15 Good Foot
16-20 Some of My Best Friends
21 & 22 Power House
23-27 Big Screamin McGrew
28 & 29 Billy Colwell

EVERY SUNDAY
HAPPY HOUR 4—8 P.M.
LIVE MUSIC
With HARRY SANDLER
Original Folk-Blues
GAME ROOM & BAR
DOWNSTAIRS

[September 1974]

[April 1974]

WESTERN FRONT

Thurs. May 14
CHRISTOPHER JONES & THE REGULARS

Fri. & Sat. May 15 & 16
LENKY ROY & THE ETHIOPIAN ROOTS

Thurs. May 21
MARIAN STREET PEOPLE BAND

Fri. & Sat. May 22 & 23
HEALIN' OF THE NATION

Sun. & Mon. May 24 & 25
DECODERS

Weds. & Thurs., May 27 & 28
MAGIC with THE REGGAE STARS

Fri. & Sat., May 29 & 30
PEACEFUL FLIGHT

Featuring: **Armstead Christian**, Vocals;
Tim Ingles, Bass; **Jim Brough**, Keyboards;
Vinnie Johnson, Drums; **SA Davis**, Percussion; **George King**, Saxophone; **Jeff Lockhart**, Guitar.

343 Western Ave Cambridge
Western & Putnam Aves.
Call For Entertainment Info
492-7772

[May 1981]

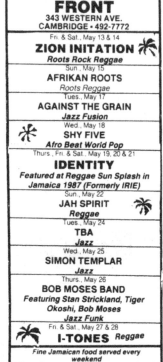

THE WESTERN FRONT
343 WESTERN AVE.
CAMBRIDGE • 492-7772

Fri. & Sat., May 13 & 14
ZION INITATION
Roots Rock Reggae

Sun., May 15
AFRIKAN ROOTS
Roots Reggae

Tues., May 17
AGAINST THE GRAIN
Jazz Fusion

Wed., May 18
SHY FIVE
Afro Beat World Pop

Thurs., Fri. & Sat., May 19, 20 & 21
IDENTITY
Featured at Reggae Sun Splash in Jamaica 1987 (Formerly IRIE)

Sun., May 22
JAH SPIRIT
Reggae

Tues., May 24
TBA
Jazz

Wed., May 25
SIMON TEMPLAR
Jazz

Thurs., May 26
BOB MOSES BAND
Featuring Stan Strickland, Tiger Okoshi, Bob Moses
Jazz Funk

Fri. & Sat., May 27 & 28
I-TONES   *Reggae*

Fine Jamaican food served every weekend

[May 1988]

Concert flyer
July 1977
[David Bieber Archives]

Miss Black Fox contestants page
May 27, 1973

[Kay Bourne Archives at Emerson College:
Iwasaki Library, Special Collections.]

Kim Bennett
19
Singing, Sports

Jeanette Blount
21
Sports, Sewing, Dancing

Tamao Sato Brevard
20
Modeling, Hairstyling

Valesay P. Cherie
21
Yoga, Karate, Swimming,
Dancing, Singing

Dorothy M. Hampton
25
Horseback Riding, Tennis,
Bowling

Jonnie Hammonds
21
Horsback Riding

Auguste Hardley
19

Deborah Howard
19

Linda Johnson
19
Travel, Dance, Horseback
Riding

Addie Kellogg
25
Sewing, Reading

Andria King
19
Tennis, Modeling, Surfing,
and Painting

Antoinette Lacefield
19
Tennis, Dancing
Professionally

Julia Morrison
21
Swimming, Cooking,
Reading, Dancing

Geraldine Pina
30
Bowling, Music & Dancing

Mattie Robinson
18

Lynda Solomon
23
Traveling & Socializing

GENE'S SLAX—Off white, sizes 7/8 & 13/14.
Were $21, **Now $10**

HALTER—Black, white, pink, orange, beige. Sizes S, M, L.
Was $6, **Now $4**

MONA—On her way to 'play' in Terry Cloth outfit.
THE SLAX Were $16,
Now only $10
THE TANK TOP was $12,
Now only $7
THE JACKET was $16,
Now only $9

· GENE'S SKIRT—Comes in an assortment of colors & styles. Sizes 5/6 to 15/16.
Were $19, **Now $12**
21, **Now $10**
17, **Now $6**
13, **Now $5**

YOUR FASHION HOROSCOPE READS: *Check out Gemini today!*

FASHIONS
2285 WASHINGTON STREET, ROXBURY, MASSACHUSETTS
Store Hours: Mon. - Thurs. & Sat. 9:30 - 6
FRIDAY 9:30 - 7

The Sporting Life newspaper
May 19, 1977
[Kay Bourne Archives at Emerson College: Iwasaki Library, Special Collections.]

Celebrity Awards Program ad
October 1982
[Kay Bourne Archives at Emerson College: Iwasaki Library, Special Collections.]

Have A

FLASH ATTACK

with: Kevin Fleetwood
"The Cadillac of Sound"
for: Musical Entertainment Services
"We are recordable, portable and affordable"
Call: 445-1217 (eve's) 296-6060 (days)

Double Exposure Studio

PHOTOGRAPHERS
Studio – Weddings – General

10 WARREN ST.
ROXBURY, MA 02119
(617) 427-8815

ROBERT HOWARD
Manager

Celebrity Awards program ad
October 1982

[Kay Bourne Archives at Emerson
College: Iwasaki Library, Special
Collections.]

**The Media Workshop
Studio/Gallery Inc.**
"A Revolutionary Concept in the Arts"
367 Boylston St., Boston 247-9234
Sat., Nov. 28 9 PM
"Tekno Groove Night"
PUPPET RULERS/MEN IN VOLTS
*First 100 people get Honorary
Memberships in "The Bottle Club"*
featuring TOM LANE & ALBERT-O
(Debut Dec. 12)
Sun., Nov. 29 3 pm
All Ages Matinee
ARSON SQUAD/JERRY'S KIDS
F.U.'S/THE FREEZE
Thurs., Dec. 3 9 pm
CUPIWE/OOH, AH, AH/WATUSI MODE
Wed., Dec. 2 8:30 pm
"New Day Film Festival"
Prize Winning Shorts & Films Every Wed. 8:30
Theatre, Gallery, Multi-Purpose rooms are available
for parties, workshops, lectures, etc. Artists, musi-
cians, apply now for studio memberships!
Listen to WMBR for Music Listings

[November & December
1981]

"Nice Dreams is a legalized high. . . . The most ambitious film yet from this outrageous duo."
– Fred Yager
Associated Press

CHEECH & CHONG'S
NICE DREAMS

Now Playing

IT'S SCENTSATIONAL!

"POLYESTER offers more honest laughs than 'Airplane'... ODORAMA™ is a wondrous screen gimmick."
— Richard Corliss/ TIME MAGAZINE

"Hilarious! POLYESTER is a salacious soap opera... Middle America run amuck."
—David Ansen
NEWSWEEK

filmed in
ODORAMA
SMELLING IS BELIEVING

Polyester

Starring DIVINE and TAB HUNTER
Written, Produced, and Directed by JOHN WATERS
A NEW LINE CINEMA PRODUCTION [R]

Starts Friday June 12th

Real Paper
June 18, 1981
[David Bieber Archives]

Celebrity Awards program ad
October 1982
[Kay Bourne Archives at Emerson College:
Iwasaki Library, Special Collections.]

You're much too beautiful to just let anyone do your hair.

Daddy's   His and Hers · 229 Mass. Ave., Boston · (617) 266-6022

If giving you 650 things to do with your eyes, ears, mouth & mind makes us an activist paper

call us an activist paper

Call us what you like. But things are happening in Boston. Things that Boston After Dark thinks you shouldn't miss out on.

Like the 62 new films, plays and art exhibits to see in the Boston area. And now some in Providence too.

And the 92 places to hear music and concerts.

And the 12 children's workshops where your child can learn how to dance, or act, or make collages, or use a camera.

That's about what you'll find in any given issue of Boston After Dark. 650 things to do and many of them free. We think it's important to open your eyes and your mind to what's going on in this city. And we do a lot to get you into things.

We get you into all the sights and sounds of the city.

We give you a taste of the greatest eating places, from Cambridge to the North End.

And we give you a lot to think about. A political talk by Daniel Ellsberg. A tenants' meeting in Dorchester. 72 health groups. 8 places to turn for recycling waste. 10 free schools where you can get into art, trout fishing, or finish your high school education. And much more. Like 1000 of the most interesting classified ads in the city.

Put more of Boston into your life. And do it now, while you can call the shots.

SAVE $5.00 off the newsstand price. I wish to subscribe to Boston After Dark for one year at the special low price of $7.50.

Name _____

Address _____

City _____ State _____ Zip _____

BOSTON after dark

Subscription Dept., 1108 Boylston St., Boston, Mass 02215

Nebula magazine

January 1972

[David Bieber Archives]

BEDFORD   FRAMINGHAM   HYANNIS   MARSHFIELD   RAYNHAM   SWAMPSCOTT
CANTON   FRANKLIN   LEOMINSTER   MEDFORD   READING   TEWKSBURY
CHELMSFORD   HINGHAM   MARLBORO   NEWTON   SOUTH WEYMOUTH   WATERTOWN
DANVERS

Over 200 stores to serve you nationwide

Fall '85

New fashion values
every week at
20% to 60% off
department store
regular prices.

In a world where
the best things in life often come
with an equally impressive price tag...
there's Marshalls.
Brand names for less.

Marshalls
Brand names for less.

Boston Phoenix
September 10, 1985
[David Bieber Archives]

Emerald Travel
Is Proud to Sponsor
The 3rd Annual
Miss Caribbean-American
Queen Pageant

Our Theme:
GLOBAL CARNIVAL

John Hancock Auditorium
200 Berkeley Street
Boston, MA
Saturday, November 5, 1988

Presented By
ACADEMY MODELING AND TALENT AGENCY
128A Tremont Street - Boston, MA 02108

Miss Carribean-American Queen Pageant program front cover

November 5, 1988

[Kay Bourne Archives at Emerson College: Iwasaki Library, Special Collections.]

Complete Play-by-Play Instructions

No errors. The computer itself coaches you, one base at a time.

It's called Computer-Based Instruction. After about an hour, you'll know the complete score.

Digital Equipment Corporation, the world's second largest computer company, not only builds superb coaching into its personal computers, it also offers an all star lineup of application software packages. Plus great moves in the craftsmanship and engineering departments.

But what else would you expect from the MVP in personal computing?

Find out how easy it is to use one of Digital's personal computers. Call 1-800 DIGITAL. Or write: Digital Equipment Corporation, 200 Baker Avenue, Concord, MA 01742.

Digital Equipment Corporation

Red Sox Yearbook

1984

[Author's Collection]

ROBOT -O- GRAMS ™
AN AFFORDABLE ROBOT THAT'S YOURS FOREVER!

Surprise someone with this amazing gift. Our remote-control, inflatable robot stands nearly 4' tall and comes dressed as a Butler, Master Chef or French Maid to serve cocktails and hors d'oeuvres or deliver the morning paper. Each robot will be personally delivered complete with uniform, hat, serving tray and champagne glasses. You may also customize your robot to fit a specific occasion (additional charge).

FANTASIES FULFILLED!

Balloons fizzle and flowers wilt, but our robots come with their own guarantee.

"Show someone you give-a-damn, Send a ROBOT-O-GRAM!"

MC/VISA $150   Call (617) 580-0131

Boston Magazine
May 1985
[David Bieber Archives]

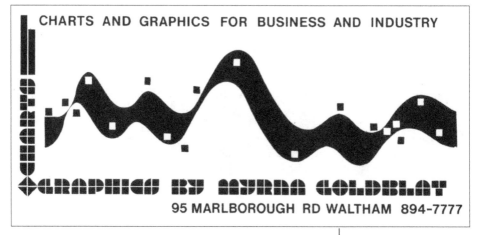

CHARTS AND GRAPHICS FOR BUSINESS AND INDUSTRY

GRAPHICS BY MYRNA GOLDBLAT
95 MARLBOROUGH RD WALTHAM 894-7777

Boston Magazine
August 1977
[Author's Collection]

DEL FUEGOS
HALF MAN TOUR '82

WED DEC 1 RANCHHOUSE MARSHFIELD w/DOGMATICS
THURS DEC 2 BOB'S PLACE w/DOGMATICS
FRI DEC 3 RAT w/NEATS
SAT DEC 4 CANTONES w/CLASSIC RUINS
SUN DEC 5 RANCHOUSE w/DOGMATICS
MON DEC 6 SPIT WERS BENEFIT

WED DEC 8 JUMPIN' JACK FLASH

Concert flyer

December 1982

[Wayne Valdez Archives]

HARPER'S FERRY

[June 1987]

SOUND MUSEUM BENEFIT - SUNDAY JUNE 28 3PM-2AM
4PM - LIMITED PARTNERSHIP, 5PM EZ RIDER, 6PM -
TRAVEL MUG, 7PM I BEFORE E, 8PM CANDY WORM
(ex-ASSASSIN), 9PM SONS OF SAPPHO, 10PM IDIOT
SAVANT, 11PM PRIME MOVERS, 12AM THE BAGS

**Concert Line 254-7380
158 Brighton Ave., Allston, MA**

We've taken the Park out of Fenway.

Our convenient Park-and-Ride lots (shown on the map in red) make it easy for you to get to the game without bringing your car into the thick of things. Just get on the T and we'll bring you right to Kenmore Square and home again. It's faster, safer, more sensible and less nervewracking than driving. Cheaper, too—and you can ride for just 10¢ during Dime Time, 10 to 2 Monday through Friday and all day Sunday on our rapid transit lines. **the answer**

Red Sox game program ad
1975
[Author's Collection]

Boston Phoenix

November 15, 1977

[David Bieber Archives]

Red Sox Yearbook

1983

[Author's Collection]

Home of Boston's Red Sox fans, critics, etc.
quick, friendly waitress service

476 Common-
wealth Avenue
Kenmore Square
Boston - 247-9712
Open 7 AM - 2 AM

OVER 300 ITEMS
ON OUR
NATIONAL AWARD-
WINNING MENU.

Eggs Served
18 Hours a Day
Fabulous
Ice Cream Desserts

TAKE OUT ANY ORDER

ROSCOE'S
"The Total Entertainment Complex"
38 WARREN STREET — ROXBURY, MA

— Proudly Presents A —

Thanksgiving ★
Weekend (Gone WILD)
★ Showdown ★

— Featuring —

HYPE-R-TENSION
Thurs. - Fri. - Sat.
NOV. 26th - 27th - 28th

2 Shows Nightly - 10 p.m. & 12 Midnight

———— EXTRA ADDED ATTRACTION ————

Special Thanksgiving Presentation
"BOSTON'S COMING OUT TO SINGLES NIGHT"
Thursday November 26 9 p.m. - 2 a.m.

Hors D'oeuvres - Champagne - Roses - Hype-R-Tension
and DISCO Extroadinaire

THIS IS A SOULFUL "T" PRODUCTION

Concert flyer

November 1981

[Kay Bourne Archives at Emerson College:
Iwasaki Library, Special Collections.]

AAMARP

IS HONORED TO PRESENT...

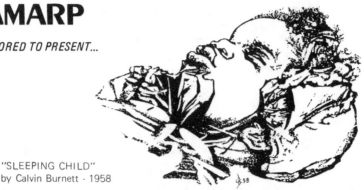

"SLEEPING CHILD"
by Calvin Burnett - 1958

A 41 YEAR RETROSPECTIVE 1939 1980
OF THE FABULOUS PAINTINGS, DRAWINGS, PRINTS, WATERCOLORS
AND AIRBRUSH IMAGES OF THE
INTERNATIONALLY REKNOWNED AAMARP ARTIST/EDUCATOR/AUTHOR

CALVIN BURNETT!
FEBRUARY 17-MARCH 14, 1980

AAMARP hours 10-4, Monday thru Sunday — Tour groups and children welcome!
11 Leon St., Northeastern University, (corner of Leon & Ruggles Sts.), Roxbury, MA 02115

COME HONOR PROFESSOR CALVIN BURNETT
AT THE
OPENING RECEPTION
WITH ALL THE AAMARP FAMILY
ON
FEB. 17th, 2 until 7 pm

FEATURING:
THE FANTASTIC CHARLIE COX TRIO! (at 2:15 in the Ryder Multi-Purpose Room)
(Charlie Cox is on the teaching faculty of Berklee College of Music, has accompanied Johnny Mathis, the Supremes, Dinah Washington, etc., and has worked with Duke Ellington, Count Basie and many others — Don't miss him!)

AND: **"THE NEW WORLD ENSEMBLE"** *RETURNS!!*
ALSO **"STEPPING INTO TOMORROW"**
A video production commemorating Black History Month (Linda Marshall, Prod. — Nina Calbazana, Asst. Prod.)

THIS EXHIBITION WILL BE CO-SPONSORED BY THE NORTHEASTERN UNIVERSITY
AFFIRMATIVE ACTION OFFICE
DEAN ELLEN JACKSON, DIRECTOR

Gallery Hours 10-4 Monday through Sunday
Sponsored by the African American Master Artists in Residency Program
(AAMARP) of Northeastern University
Refresnments served
Curator, Dana Chandler

Free and Open to the Public at All Times
Printing courtesy of AAMARP of Northeastern University,
Professor Dana Chandler, Creator-Director
Dean Jim Reed, Co-Director

Event flyer

February 1980

[Kay Bourne Archives at Emerson College: Iwasaki Library, Special Collections.]

Axe' Experimental Theatre
Director: Carnell Coley
298-1790

Featuring:

Carnell Coley..Dancer, Singer, Percussionist
Nassim Abbul-Malik...Saxophone
Patrick Lacroise (of Haiti)...Singer, Dancer
Mastre Deraldo Ferreira (of Brazil)..............................Dancing, Singing, Percussionist

Special Guest

Anderson Castro...Singing and Dancing
David Sandzer...Singing, Drumming
Brandon Guillermo..Singing and Drummer

Miss Carribean American Queen
Pageant program ad
November 5, 1988

[Kay Bourne Archives at Emerson College:
Iwasaki Library, Special Collections.]

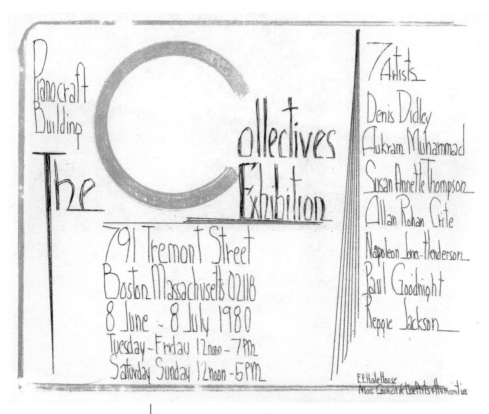

Art Exhibit flyer

June / July 1980

[Kay Bourne Archives at Emerson College:
Iwasaki Library, Special Collections.]

Night Life magazine
February 1974
[David Bieber Archives]

Event program (front and back covers)
October 1981
[Kay Bourne Archives at Emerson College: Iwasaki Library, Special Collections.]

Concert poster
October 1976
[David Bieber Archives]

BUZZARD MOTORCYCLE CLUB INC.

PRESENT THEIR

Gala Spring Trophy Run

Saturday, May 21, 1977

9:00 P.M. UNTIL

BROMLEY HEATH HALL

10 LAMARTINE ST. — JAMAICA PLAIN, MA

TICKETS $5 ADVANCE $6 AT DOOR

FOR INFORMATION CALL
427-9063

The Sporting Life
newspaper
May 19, 1977

[Kay Bourne Archives
at Emerson College:
Iwasaki Library, Special
Collections.]

BRANDY'S I

WHERE INCREDIBLE
FRIENDSHIPS BEGIN

1110 Commonwealth Ave.
617-232-4386

For Feb.

Clean Livin

Bad Saloon

Fat

East West Journal
February 1974
[David Bieber Archives]

NIGHTSTAGE

Best Nightclub 1986 — *Boston Magazine*

Sat., Oct. 25 • 9:00 & 11:30
from L.A. blues doubleheader
EDDIE "CLEANHEAD" VINSON
and **LOWELL FULSON**
David Maxwell
& The Blues Survivors

Tues., Oct. 28 • 7:30 & 10:30
ASLEEP AT THE WHEEL
MEMPHIS ROCKABILLY

Wed., Oct. 29 • 9:00 & 11:00
ROOMFUL OF BLUES

Thurs., Oct. 30 • 8:00 & 11:00
from Nashville
WDLW
JOHNNY PAYCHECK
AND THE WORKINGMAN'S BAND
Larry Flint

Fri., Oct. 31
celebrate Halloween with
BIG TWIST AND THE MELLOW FELLOWS

Sat., Nov. 1
DUKE ROBILLARD
AND THE PLEASURE KINGS

Sun., Nov. 2 • 7:00 & 10:00
an evening with
GIL SCOTT-HERON
and "dub poet"
LINTON KWESI JOHNSON

Tues. & Wed., Nov. 4 & 5
7:30 & 10:30
SUN RA
AND HIS ARKESTRA
with special guest
PHIL ALVIN
from **THE BLASTERS**

Thurs. - Sat., Nov. 6 - 8
8:00 & 11:00
ETTA JAMES
and **OTIS CLAY**
HI-RHYTHM SECTION

Tues., Nov. 11
UNCLE BONSAI

Thurs., Nov. 13 • 7:30 & 10:30
Windham Hill Recording Artists
MONTREUX
featuring
**DAROL ANGER, MIKE MARSHALL,
BARBARA HIGBIE, MICHAEL MANRING**

Sat., Nov. 15 • 8:00 & 11:00
PIECES OF A DREAM

Tues., Nov. 18
WORLD SAXOPHONE QUARTET

Coming
Nov 23   Robert Cray Band

R·O·S·E·M·A·R·Y
RESTAURANT
Located downstairs from Nightstage
Dinner/Show Special!!
Half price admission to Nightstage
with dinner
By reservation only — Call 497-7200
Open for lunch Mon. - Fri. 11:30 - 3:00
Dinner Tues. - Sat. 5:00 - 11:00

823 Main St., Camb., Mass.

For ticket info. call 497-8200 or Concert Charge 497-1118, Teletron 720-3434 or all Ticketron locations
• All Strawberries locations • Live entertainment nightly • Valet parking available
• Open Sun - Wed 8 p m til 1 a m Thurs Sat til 2 a m

[October & November 1986]

[November 1977]

at Michael's Pub

Mon.	**Fringe**
Tues.	**David Jackson & Friends**
Wed.	**Jackie Byard and The Apollo Stompers**
Thurs.-Sat.	**Sorcery**
Sun.	**Open Jam**

The finest jazz that Boston has to offer, seven nights a week
52A Gainsboro St. Boston
247-7262

*Elite Designers
program ad*

September 13, 1981

[Kay Bourne Archives
at Emerson College:
Iwasaki Library, Special
Collections.]

CHEZ - VOUS ROLLERWAY

11 RHOADES STREET
DORCHESTER, MA 02124

Tel. 1-617-825-6877

Joseph Waters, Manager

The Sporting Life newspaper

May 19, 1977

[Kay Bourne Archives at Emerson College:
Iwasaki Library, Special Collections.]

Estelle's

888 Tremont St. Boston

427-0200

Thurs. Mens Night

BELLYGRAMS:

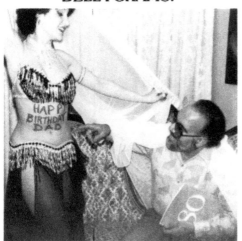

MOVING MESSAGES
FOR
MOVING HOLIDAYS

(or any other occasions)
Odalisque Studios Ltd. trains bellydancers at all levels—Give an
Odalisque Gift Certificate this season. Call for brochure.

ODALISQUE
1902 Mass. Ave.
Cambridge, MA.
661-8508

Boston Magazine

December 1980

[David Bieber Archives]

Mavericks
Tekno
Groove

Thu 18 Grand Opening *from NYC...* **LIQUID LIQUID**
Fri 18 **PRIMARY COLORS** **LIMBO RACE**
Sat 20 **THE DARK** **YOUNG SNAKES**
Thu 25 **M.I.A.'S** **ZODIO DOZE**
Fri 26 **PETER DAYTON** **STRIPPER**
Sat 27 **BOYS LIFE** **007**
Thu & Fri, March 4 & 5 *only area appearance...* **FLIPPER** *(advance tix at Newbury Comics)*
Sat 6 *from Philly...* **BUNNYDRUMS**
Sat 13 *from D.C. ...* **TINY DESK UNITS**
112 BROAD ST. **423-4333** **advance tix sold at Newbury Comics**

[February & March 1982]

Take It! magazine

1981

[Author's Collection]

BLACK PEOPLES' ASSOCIATION OF GREATER BOSTON

IN A BENEFIT FOR

THE BLACK PEOPLES' CULTURAL ARTS FESTIVAL

PRESENTS

THE ELMA LEWIS SCHOOL OF FINE ARTS PERFORMING TROUPE

Featuring: PRIMITIVE DANCE
MUSIC
BLACK POETRY
MATTIE MANGRAM, SINGER

Friday, May 22, 1970, 8:00 P.M.

AT

NORTHEASTERN UNIVERSITY ALUMNI AUDITORIUM

360 HUNTINGTON AVE.

Tickets: A Nubian Notion,
Northeastern University Afro Am Center

$1.50 — $2.00 at the door

Event flyer

May 1970

[Kay Bourne Archives at Emerson College:
Iwasaki Library, Special Collections.]

[June 1988]

Elite Designers
program ad

September 13, 1981

[Kay Bourne Archives
at Emerson College:
Iwasaki Library, Special
Collections.]

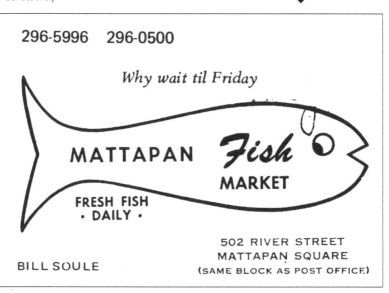

Boston Advertiser
Nov 24, 1963
[Author's collection]

THE BOSTON TEA PARTY
53 berkeley street

dec 15 & 16
richie havens
the bagatelle

dec 22 & 23
lothar & the hand people
the beacon street union

The Avatar

December 8, 1967

[David Bieber Archives]

Boston Rock magazine

August 1980

[David Bieber Archives]

Photo: Kathy Chapman

DO YOU REMEMBER ROCK & ROLL RADIO?

THE LATE RISERS CLUB   MON-FRI 9 A.M. to 1 P.M.
returning August 4th on WMBR 88.1 FM

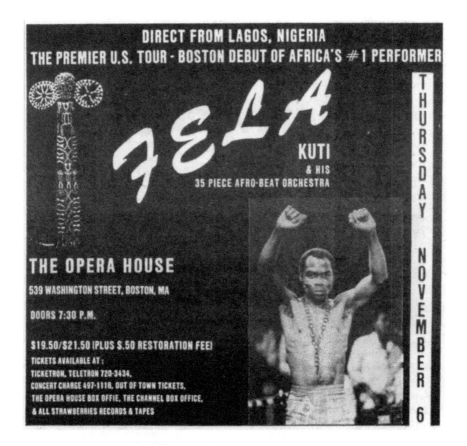

Boston Phoenix
October 28, 1986
[David Bieber Archives]

Boston Phoenix

December 1, 1981

[David Bieber Archives]

NEW BLACK PLAY
WORLD PREMIERE

CANT
KILL
NOTHING
AND
WONT
NOTHING
DIE

WRITTEN BY DONALD LESTER
DIRECTED BY SUMNER McCLAINE

Sat. & Sun. April 29-30 8 PM
Then, Fridays & Saturdays 8 PM

Tickets $2.50
Reservations Phone 547-4930

New Theatre in Cambridge

PEOPLES THEATRE

1253 Cambridge St.   near Inman Square

PEOPLES THEATRE IS SPONSORED BY THE CAMBRIDGE YWCA

Event flyer

April 1972

[Kay Bourne Archives at Emerson College:
Iwasaki Library, Special Collections.]

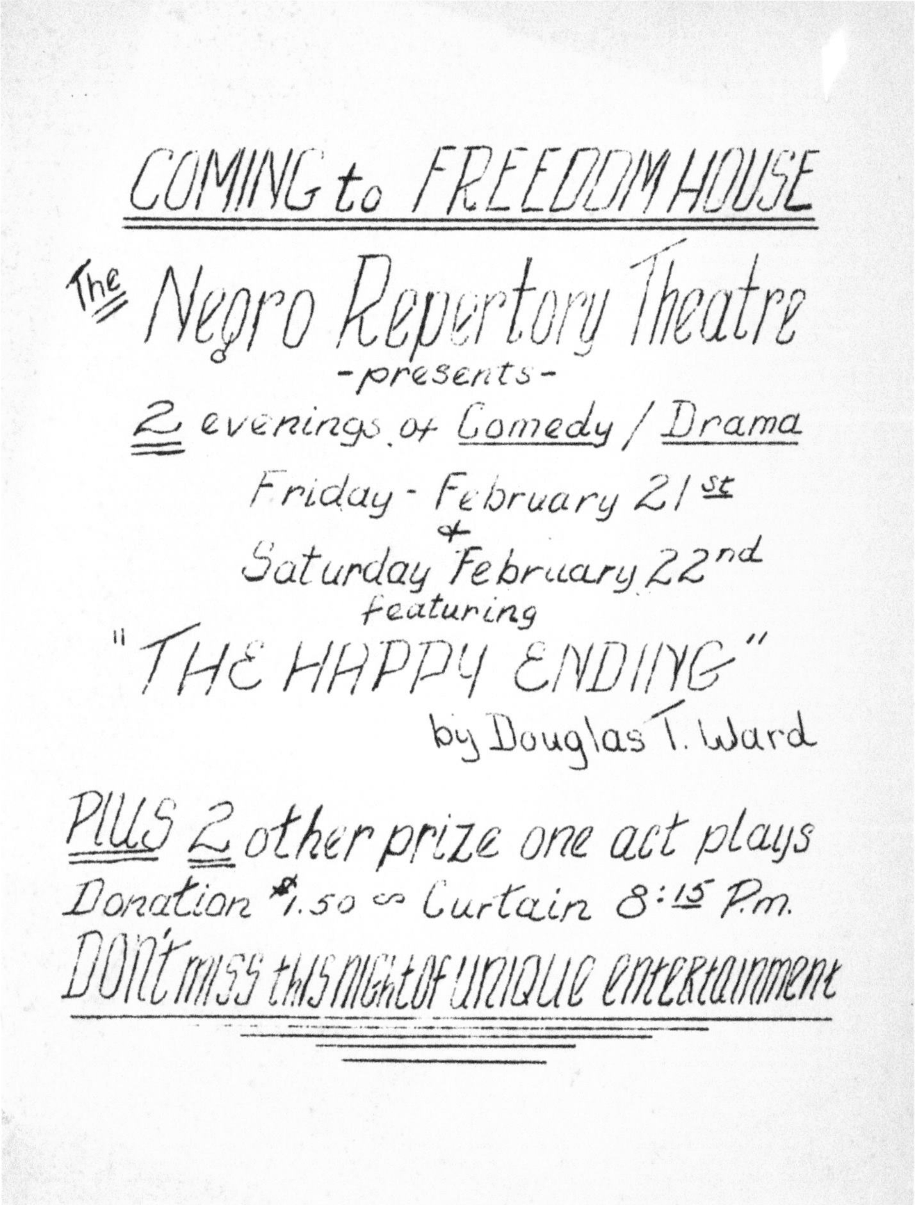

Event flyer

1969 [most likely]

[Kay Bourne Archives at Emerson College:
Iwasaki Library, Special Collections.]

Boston Music Group

Box 477, Boston, Ma. 02215   (617) 884-6442

LIVE LOBSTER

Boston's Fastest Rising
Rock Band
5 Band Members
Complete Sound & Light
System with Operators

DEAD END KIDS

Incredibly Tight 4 pc Unit
Seeped in Recording &
Touring Experience
Great Dance Band

ORCHESTRA LUNA

A Serious Assortment of
Significant Smilers. New LP on
Epic. Smash Cncert Act

ALSO

MAD ANGEL

PHLUPH

CHRIS MARTIN GROUP

HOBO TOAD

GARBO

CARNABY

BACK STREET BEAT

MOUNT ZION

PRISM

ANNIE HACKETT

SLIPPERY ELM

KICK BACK

REDDY TEDDY

KUPA KUPA

ADRIAN

JOHN LINCOLN WRIGHT &

THE SOURASH BOYS

SLEDGE HAMMA

THUNDER TRAIN

AMERICAN STANDARD

"Book Your Proms and Parties Early"

Night Time magazine

March 1975

[David Bieber Archives]

Highland Tap Room

2nd SMASH WEEK

The Dynamic

Arthur Davis Group

(formerly Different Strokes)

BACK BY POPULAR DEMAND
STARTING WEDNESDAY MARCH 24

MARGO THUNDER

Appearing every Monday night,
Listen to the Disco Sounds of

MR. JELLY BELLY
& THE PUSSY CAT REVIEW

Featuring the beautiful and exotic
Red Robin

Daily Breakfasts $.99 and Under
Daily Luncheon Specials
Featuring chicken & ribs

Happy Hour
Mon. thru Sat. 10 a.m.-8 p.m
All Drinks Discounted

Bostons Cleanest Finest Deli

2128 WASHINGTON ST.
Tel. 427-6514

Bay State Banner

March 1976

[Kay Bourne Archives at Emerson College: Iwasaki Library, Special Collections.]

Night Life magazine

April 1975

[David Bieber Archives]

CHAUNCEYS of So. Boston

77-79 DORCHESTER ST.
TEL. 617-268-2119

APR. 15–APR. 27
Cook Book
APR. 29–MAY 4
Good Feelin'
MAY 6–MAY 18
ON STAGE

Cook Book

So. Boston's Greatest Show Club
MANY STAR ATTRACTIONS TO FOLLOW

**BOSTON UNIVERSITY
PRESENTS**

THE WHO

*In Concert
Performing*
" TOMMY OPERA "
plus
" THE FLOCK "
COMMONWEALTH ARMORY
FRIDAY NIGHT OCTOBER 10
8:30p.m.
TICKETS $ 4, $ 3, $ 2

*Boston After
Dark*

October 1, 1969

[David Bieber
Archives]

SATURDAY NIGHT OCTOBER 11

RICHIE HAVENS

SARGENT GYM

8:30 PM   TICKETS $2.50

TICKETS AVAILABLE
FOR BOTH CONCERTS
AT
GSU TICKET OFFICE 353-3651
OR
OUT OF TOWN TICKET AGENCY
HARVARD SQUARE
OR
AT THE DOOR

Groups HIT CITY 24 Tracks   *Singers HIT CITY 24 Tracks*

HIT CITY RECORDING STUDIO

can put your music on wax

HIT CITY is Boston's Newest 24-track "State-of-the-Art" Studio
Gospel, Rap, Jazz, Reggae, Funk, Dance Music Productions

HIT CITY RECORDING STUDIO

features a complete record release service. Our professional staff will handle your entire project from songwriting to production to mastering to pressing. You'll receive 1000 records in just six weeks and free marketing consultation.

For FURTHER INFORMATION or STUDIO BOOKINGS, call: (617) 442-8721

Rappers HIT CITY 24-Tracks   *Musicians HIT CITY 24 Tracks*

Tony Rose   Sidney Burton
Managing Director   Chief Engineer

*Miss Carribean American Queen
Pageant program ad*

November 5, 1988

[Kay Bourne Archives at Emerson College:
Iwasaki Library, Special Collections.]

Concert flyer

December 1987

[David Bieber Archives / Chuck White]

Boston Phoenix

November 15, 1977

[David Bieber Archives]

Boston Phoenix

December 1, 1981

[David Bieber Archives]

1369 JAZZ CLUB

Sun., Nov. 13
ANIMATION
Plus Animation will MC
OPEN JAZZ JAM SESSION
5pm till 1am
FREE BUFFET FOR ALL
FREE BEER for
participating musicians!
Mon., Nov. 14
ELEGUA
(9-pc. latin jazz band)
Tues. & Wed.,
Nov. 15 & 16
**YOSHINO YANAGIHARA
ROSEI UCHIDA** with
BUNNY SMITH and **FRIENDS**
Thurs-.Sat., Nov. 17-19
LESTER PARKER

*Fine selection
of choice
liquors
Happy
Hour till
9 p.m.*

1369 Cambridge St
Inman Square Cambridge   **354-9059**

[November 1977]

BIJOU HIP POCKET

CLOTHING FOR
THE MALE AND FEMALE

101-103 UNION ST.
PICCADILLY SQ. NEWTON CTR.
10-6, MON., TUES., SAT.
10-9, WED., THUR., FRI.

The Real Paper

October 1, 1975

[David Bieber Archives]

CANTONES

WHERE BOSTON'S
ROCK BANDS ARE BORN

Thu 18
Shockers • Drezniak

Fri 19
Suade Cowboys • Stereotypes

Sat 20
Stealers • Bones

Wed 24
Specimens • Score • Air Raid

Thu 25
Attitude • Modes

Fri 26
TBA

Sat 27
Rampage • Agents

Wed March 3
Tynan Cross • Batik

Thu 4
Your Mother • East Wind

Fri 5
Limbo Race • Ice Age

Sat 6
Sweet Evil • Ancestor Worship

Wed 10
Ruff Cuts • Second Division

Thu 11
Score • Exports

Fri 12
Gary Shane & Detour
David Champagne's Pink Cadillacs
Solicitors

Sat 13
Suade Cowboys • Last Sacrifice

Wed 17
Square Peg • Kitch-n Sync

Thu 18
Air Raid • Racer

Fri 19
Urban Allies • 21-645 • Gluons

Sat 20
Bimbos • Psycho • Commandos

Happy Hour with Kennie Mon.-Fri. 4-7

**69 BROAD ST., BOSTON
338-7677**

For bookings, dial YELL-FUN, ask
for:
**COUNT JOE, Wed.-Sun.
TERRY, Mon. & Tues.** (call at club)

[February &
March 1982]

Jazz It Up!
at the
PAGE CAFÉ

Thurs., June 11
SPRING
Fri. & Sat., June 12 & 13
MILI BERMEJO
& MONTEZUMA's REVENGE
Sun., June 14
SPRING
Weds. & Thurs., June 17 & 18
The Unforgettable
ROBERT SILVERMAN

Every
Monday & Tuesday
GENTLEMEN & LADIES NIGHT
All Drinks $1.25
5 PM until...

Live jazz
Weds. - Sun.

- NEVER A Cover Charge
- Proper Dress Required
- Happy Hour Mon.-Fri., 5-7 PM

1667 Blue Hill Ave., Mattapan

Watch
For New
Restaurant

• • • • • • • • • • • • • •

OPENING SOON!

• • • • • • • • • • • • • •

Featuring:
Barbecued Ribs
Southern Fried
Chicken
& Seafood

[October 1978]

[June 1981]

JONATHAN SWIFTS

John Lincoln Wright .... Oct. 7th & 8th
Jeff Muldaur · Amos Garrett 9th
Randy Roos 10th
Zachariah,... 11th
Chuck McDermott
& Wheatstraw...12th 13th 14th

Woodstock Mountains
Revue...16th
Featuring: Pat Algan, Caroline Dutton, John Herald,
Billy Keith, Jim Rooney, Roly Salley, Gordon Titcomb,
Happy and Artie Traum

**FREE ADMISSION FOR THE FIRST 50 PEOPLE WITH THIS AD
OCTOBER 16th ONLY
(Space Permitting)**

Widespread Depression Orchestra,............................18th
Estes Boys..19th-21st
In Concert :   Fred Willard
America 2 Night's
Jerry Hubbard 22nd
Art Ensemble of Chicago
Anthony Braxton...23nd
Anthony Braxton
Leroy Jenkins Trio 24th
Yusaf Lateef..25th
Mose Allison..26th
Young Adults ....27th & 28th
Tom Paxton..29th
Roomful of Blues 30th-31st

30 BOYLSTON STREET, CAMBRIDGE,
MA For Further Information Call: 661-9887

LIVE ENTERTAINMENT IS OPENING AT

TINKER'S

888 Tremont Street, Boston, Mass.

Our Featured Opening Night Attraction
Will Be

HANK CRAWFORD

"Jazz Saxophonist"

Thursday, Sept. 25, 9 pm — 2 am
Sunday, Sept. 28, 7 pm — 12 pm

Special Opening Night Price — $3.00

"He sings the Blues through his horn"
  . . . *Essence Magazine*

For more information call 427-0200

Robert Tinker

Coming October 2-5   James
HOUSTON PERSON, featuring Etta ~~Jones~~

AFFORDABLE JAZZ IN THE CITY FOR YOU!!
  . . . Dress code in effect

Concert flyer

September 1980

[Kay Bourne Archives at Emerson College:
Iwasaki Library, Special Collections]

1120 BOYLSTON STREET ° BOSTON (near auditorium station)

october 23 -29

Tim Buckley

oct. 30 - nov. 5

Junior Wells

Bostons
newest
coffeehouse!

[October 1967]

[February 1974]

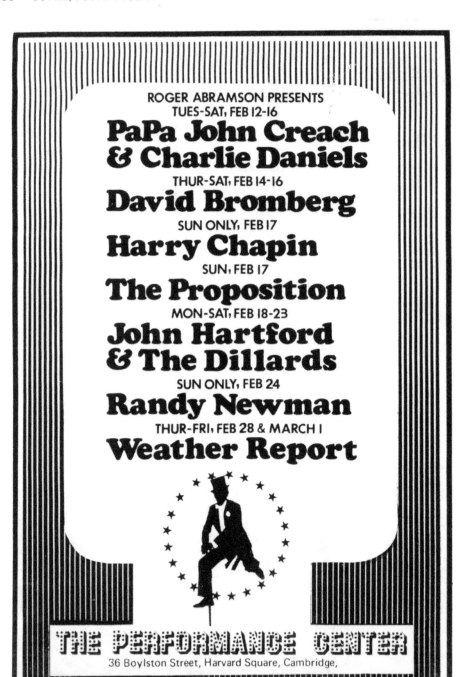

ROGER ABRAMSON PRESENTS
TUES-SAT, FEB 12-16

PaPa John Creach & Charlie Daniels

THUR-SAT, FEB 14-16

David Bromberg

SUN ONLY, FEB 17

Harry Chapin

SUN, FEB 17

The Proposition

MON-SAT, FEB 18-23

John Hartford & The Dillards

SUN ONLY, FEB 24

Randy Newman

THUR-FRI, FEB 28 & MARCH 1

Weather Report

THE PERFORMANCE CENTER

36 Boylston Street, Harvard Square, Cambridge,

[February 1974]

[May & June 1974]

[October 1969]

Broadside magazine
October 25, 1967
[David Bieber Archives]

Events flyer
July 1983
[Wayne Valdez Archives]

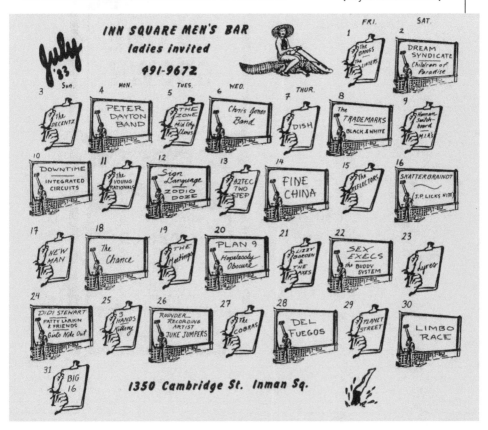

JACQUES

79 Broadway

CABARET

(Behind Howard Johnson's)
426-8902

NEW YEAR'S EVE

FOLLIES BERGERE SHOW

10 'TIL CLOSING

☆ ☆ ☆ ☆ ☆

MONDAY, JANUARY 26, 1987

9 P.M.

7TH ANNUAL

MISS GAY NEW ENGLAND CONTEST

☆ CASH PRIZE   ☆ TROPHY   ☆ CROWN

☆ NO ENTRY FEE

(Call Johnny Freda after 6 p.m. for information on categories at (617) 426-8902)

SPECIAL GUEST   MALINDA WILSON
MISS GAY NEW ENGLAND 1986

*Guide To Gay
New England*

January 1987

[Author's Collection]

Concert poster

April 1985

[Courtesy of Reebee Garofalo and UMass Boston: Massachusetts Rock Against Racism records, University Archives & Special Collections.]

LEO AND HIS BROTHER ARE BOTH FIRST STRING PLAYERS AT THE BOYS' CLUB.

Meet Leo and his brother Sam. One is learning to play shortstop. The other is learning to play cello.

You may never see Leo play at Fenway Park, or hear Sam play at Symphony Hall.

But you might. At The Boys' Clubs, we try to instill a desire to excel. One tragedy of inner-city kids is their in-bred failure orientation. So we give them something to be good at. A way to build self-esteem, pride, and a feeling of achievement. No matter what it is they like to do. And then we make them want to be great at it. Big league. Because they'll never make it if they don't believe they can.

The Boys' Clubs of Boston are doing the most for the kids who need it the most. To some kids, it's something to do. To others, it's opportunities. And to a lot of kids, it's home.

THE BOYS' CLUBS OF BOSTON
To a lot of kids, it's home.
Member United Way of Mass. Bay.

Red Sox Yearbook

1981

[Author's collection]

Boston After Dark
October 1, 1969
[David Bieber Archives]

The Boston College Social Committee and
the Arch Foundation present

DIANA ROSS and the SUPREMES

in two performances

Friday, October 3

McHugh Forum, Boston College
7:30 p.m. and 10:00 p.m.

Tickets on sale at:
Out of Town Ticket Agency, Harvard Square
McElroy Commons, Boston College
$3.50 $4.50 $5.50

the Arch Foundation   Advancing Research in Cancer and Heart

The Avatar
June 9, 1967
[David Bieber Archives]

Night Life magazine
May 1973
[David Bieber Archives]

INDEX

DESIGNER'S NOTE

Surprise: just like my partner-in-crime Brian, I'm not from Boston either.

Drove me crazy as a kid. Always felt like I was on the outside looking in. Looking back, I realize that it has actually served me well. The world would be a better place if everyone attacked their day like they have something to prove. I didn't know it at the time, but the chip I lovingly nurtured on my shoulder would actually turn me into a Bostonian – regardless of zip code.

I learned the city by skateboarding here. In the late '80s and early '90s, learning to skate in Boston (while living in the suburbs) made you a red-headed stepchild. West Concord to Porter Square, downstairs to the T. The Red Line outbound meant Z.T.'s and the C-Pool; inbound meant anything from handrails at the Charles River Hotel to the banks at City Hospital. Forget respect: if you wanted to get good lines at these spots, you had to be willing to *try* and go as big and fast as the skaters from the city. Or come back when nobody else was around.

Skaters look at the landscape a little differently than people just walking around. *"How high do I need to ollie to get over that?"* You develop a different muscle memory, too. When I walk through Copley with my kids today, my feet still remember how hard I need to push. My knees remember *exactly* how high I need to ollie.

When Brian told me about his idea for this book, I thought it sounded *pretty cool*. Then he came over with a stack of old items to photograph – only some of which you see in this edition of *Buy Me, Boston*, by the way – and the memories that came flowing back were visceral. I am almost as grateful to the people who collected all these wonderful artifacts, as I am to the artists who created them.

Working my way through the content in these pages felt like I was standing right in front of the stage, downstairs at The Middle East in 1994 – watching a truly great show unfold. I got to experience the magic of discovering this city all over again. I hope you've enjoyed it as much as I have.

James Blackwell
June 2018